The Cinderella Notes

By

Ramesh S Arunachalam

First published in December 2016 by
Shruthikka Media World through
The Createspace Independent Publishing Platform

Contact: shruthika438@gmail.com

Cover Design: Leena Swamy
Research Assistance: SP Pandyan

Copyright Information

Contents

CHAPTER 1

At the Stroke of Midnight

Cinderella: Why, it's like a dream. A wonderful dream come true.
Fairy Godmother: Yes, my child, but like all dreams, well, I'm afraid this can't last forever. You'll have only 'til midnight, and then...
Cinderella: Midnight? Oh, thank you.
Fairy Godmother: Oh, now, now, now, now, now, just a minute. You must understand, my dear: On the stroke of twelve, the spell will be broken, and everything will be as it was before.
Cinderella: Oh, I understand, but... it's more than I ever hoped for.—Source: *Cinderella*[1] **(1950 film)**

Unlike the mythical Cinderella, India's 500 and 1,000 rupee notes were not given fair warning. Cozily ensconced in the confines of Indian wallets, cash registers and safety vaults among other places, as the most cherished possessions of their holders, they had no clue what was coming their way. Occupying pride of place on the highest rungs of India's currency system, they hardly knew that the magic spell that converted them from mere pieces of paper to legal tender would wear off at midnight some day.

---

[1] *Cinderella* is a 1950 American animated musical fantasy film produced by Walt Disney, based on the fairy tale *Cendrillon* by Charles Perrault.

The Cinderella Notes

November 8, 2016, was not unlike any other day in the life of India. At the fall of dusk, most Indians retired to their homes, to spend the rest of the evening indulging in their usual pastimes that ranged from lounging in front of their television sets to browsing the net to even catching up on family time. It would soon be nightfall and most looked forward to going to bed and grabbing some sleep before it was time to wake up to the grind of a new day. The events of the day had given them no inkling of the tumult that was to come their way.

After an early dinner, I had decided to catch up on some reading and so failed to note the news that Prime Minister Narendra Modi was to address the nation shortly on national television. It was around half past eight when my wife came rushing in to break the news that the five hundred and thousand rupee notes had been demonetized and would cease to be legal tender at the stroke of midnight.

To say that I was gobsmacked would be putting it mildly. I thought she'd gotten her facts wrong and went online to check things for myself. I should have known that wives are seldom wrong. There it was, spelled in black and white and the television news, when I tuned into it, was playing clips of the announcement repeatedly. Five hundred and thousand rupee notes were indeed to suffer a sad demise at midnight. They were to be replaced by a newly designed 2000 rupee note and further down the line, by a new 500 rupee note. After the initial shock, I speed-dialed my bank manager only to discover that he was as clueless as I was. He was driving home from work and had just taken a call from a friend informing him of the same.

Here I was, a man with enough connections in the banking and financial sector, and there he was, a man within the system itself, and neither of us had had a clue. Images of a new two thousand rupee note had been floating around on social media over the past few days but nothing on demonetization, not a whiff. At least I had not smelt it!

After the initial shock, it was time to take stock of our own situation. Between my wife and me, we had just over five thousand rupees in the soon to be worthless notes, so there was no major fear there. Most of our payments were made online or through debit/credit cards and we had no use for cash beyond the few buys we made from the small vendors who were yet to join the digital financial system.

My wife decided to make a quick trip to the ATM, just so we could get hold of a few smaller denomination notes. We did have some currency that would still be valid past midnight but she decided to make the trip anyway. It seemed to me that she was curious to gauge the reactions of people around. Anyway, she came back soon enough saying that the ATMs were offering only 500 and 1,000 notes. A few customers were making multiple withdrawals of less than 500 rupees but she didn't feel it was worth the effort. The banks were to be shut the next day and the ATMs would not function for a couple of days but we had enough to see us through the time.

While there were dissenting voices even in the immediate aftermath of demonetization it must be noted that a good majority approved of the initiative. It was, after all, billed as a measure against black money[2] as well as counterfeit currency. Even political opponents had to preface their criticism with the caveat that they were all for rooting out corruption.

According to a study conducted by Ambit Capital Research,[3] the size of the black[4] economy in India stood at Rs 30 lakh crore or about 20 percent of the total GDP[5]. There was, however, no official[6] estimate on the exact amount of black money in the country. Although demonetization would attack only the cash component of the black money reserves, Prime Minister Modi's speech indicated that the

---

[2] Money/Income not reflected in the records and remaining outside the formal financial system is often referred to as black money in common parlance in India.

[3] See 'India's black economy shrinking, pegged at 20% of GDP: Report', June 5, 2016, *The Indian Express*, PTI, http://indianexpress.com/article/business/economy/ambit-capital-black-economy-shrinking-pegged-at-20-per-cent-of-gdp-2835783/

[4] Black economy refers to the parallel or shadow economy, the transactions of which are not reflected in the formal accounting system.

[5] Gross domestic product (GDP) is a monetary measure of the market value of all final goods and services produced in a period (quarterly or yearly).

[6] See 'No estimation of black money either before or after November 8: FM Arun Jaitley', December 16, 2016, *The Economic Times*, PTI, http://economictimes.indiatimes.com/news/economy/finance/no-estimation-of-black-money-either-before-or-after-november-8-fm-arun-jaitley/articleshow/56019908.cms

move was akin to blowing the war bugle, the equivalent of the first attack that would take the enemy flanks by surprise. Although the government had been making incremental efforts to address the black money menace, this was the first overt strike at such scale.

If social media reactions to the announcement were to be taken as a measure of the people's pulse, they were tired of a system that allowed rampant corruption, black marketeering, hoarding and tax evasion to prevail. They wanted the cycle to be broken, they wanted change.

In the days that followed, change became the buzzword, albeit in a different sense. For people were literally left scrambling around for change in the form of smaller denomination notes, as opposed to the new 2,000 rupee notes that were almost impossible to break.

The days following demonetization put even the diehard optimists to test. A cash strapped population was left waiting, for days on end at times, in front of banks and ATMs, and thousands of human hours were lost as a result. Further, essential services were denied to people in places, despite the government's notification that the demonetized currency would continue to be legal tender in select outlets like government run hospitals, pharmacies and petrol bunks among others. And the informal economy, comprising the small traders, street vendors and others, was thrown completely out of gear. While any such far-reaching decision is bound to cause collateral damage, the knowledge does not make it any easier to digest it.

A multitude of thoughts flitted through my mind as I sat observing the events that unfolded: the responses, the disappointments, the pitfalls; and yet, it seemed to me that it was presumptuous to write off the far reaching consequences and benefits that an audacious and courageous decision such as this could yield. This is because the decision appeared to have been taken in a bid to fulfill an election promise and yet, it had the potential to eat into political capital.

Looking beyond the immediate, I felt that the demonetization decision can indeed be a game changer for the Indian economy, but not in isolation. While it can serve as a trigger, it needs to be backed up by a series of forward looking measures if we are to have any hope of reaping the rewards of this move and be convinced that the interim hardships are worth it. It is another matter that some of these hardships could have been mitigated to some extent, if not completely avoided. However, the deed was done and the pragmatist in me felt the need now was to adopt a forward stance.

I decided to put my thoughts on paper: my perspective on the bold demonetization measure, its impact and the ways forward, as seen through the prism of my experiences working in the informal and unorganized sector including with MSMEs, (digital) financial inclusion and micro/rural finance, financial services including their regulation and supervision, urban development, media and entertainment and also macro level planning/ consulting. Over the last three decades, my work has exposed me to the ground realities of close to 570 of India's 600 plus districts and there are some valuable insights that I have been privileged enough to gain in the process.

In keeping with my motto of 'never backward, always forward', I devote the bulk of the book to a discussion of the additional measures that need to be implemented and opportunities that need to be seized if the demonetization move is to truly benefit the Indian economy in the long run. The book, however, would be an incomplete effort if I did not offer a fair assessment of the immediate fallout of the demonetization decision and its impact on the people. In doing this, I also highlight strategies that might have served to minimize the pain as well as underscore key lessons from this experience.

For the sake of convenience, I have adopted a sector-wise approach in my analysis of existing conditions, the impact of demonetization and the slew of measures that need to be adopted so that the benefits of this exercise can truly be long-term. Without these, demonetization will remain a temporary measure that addresses the symptoms alone, and not the causative factors, and will result in the resurfacing of 'black money' after a brief period of remission.

The book unfolds as follows:

Chapter 2—*Down The Rabbit Hole*—focuses on the fallout of the demonetization move and its immediate consequences for the Indian people. It attempts to delineate steps that might have helped deal with the consequent snafus. It offers a historical perspective on demonetization and sheds light on the opportunities that the move could well trigger for the Indian economy.

Chapter 3—*Cracking The Digital Code*—takes a hard look at the existing digital finance infrastructure in a bid to assess its capacity and preparedness to service growing needs. It suggests required scaling up measures, to be undertaken on priority, if there is to be a painless transition to the cashless, digital economy. It also describes the incentives and measures that would be needed to bring into the digital finance fold those people who have hitherto not been a part of the digital finance revolution.

Chapter 4—*The Realty Show*—looks at the causative factors for the real estate sector being the single largest source of black money fuelled transactions. It suggests practical ways in which they can be eliminated. These are among the most crucial steps that need implementation if the demonetization effort is to have any real meaning. In the wake of demonetization, turbocharging the economy is crucial and the role of the real estate sector acquires even greater significance given its huge contributions to the national and state GDPs.

Chapter 5—*To Pay Or Not To Pay*—explores the income tax conundrum and suggests practical ways in which India's tax system can be rationalized to eliminate black money generation. The need is to move from the existing complex income tax system to one that is simple, cost effective and transparent with lower transaction costs and greater ease of operation for both the government and the taxpayer. The chapter also examines practical ways in which the existing/accumulated black money reserves—whether in India or abroad and/or stored in other forms like real estate, jewels, stocks, shares etc.–can be mopped up without a loss to the exchequer through the prudent use of fiscal and other incentives.

Chapter 6—*The Building Blocks*—outlines ways in which the primary building blocks on which the country's economy rests, namely the agriculture, manufacturing and services sectors, can be strengthened and resources appropriately deployed to trigger growth at a rapid pace and to create more jobs with a view to pushing more people out of poverty.

Chapter 7—*Taming the Corrupt*—focuses on the steps that need to be taken to fight spectacular and day-to-day corruption from a practical standpoint. It also looks at one of the key areas of spectacular corruption which concerns the arbitrary manner in which 'natural resource allocation' has occurred in India to the detriment of the large majority of Indians.

Chapter 8—*Dirty Money*—delves into the issue of the funding of political parties and suggests practical ways in which the same can be made transparent and accountable, from the perspective of the people of India.

Chapter 9—*The Beginning*—is the conclusion which summarizes the six small practical steps that need to be immediately implemented if we are to realize long term benefits from this bold de-monetization measure. Put differently, failure to implement these now could mean that demonetization may well end up becoming the much dreaded speed breaker for the Indian economy that had hitherto been growing at a reasonable pace.

Appendices—contain relevant data and material supportive of the arguments made in the main chapters.

CHAPTER 2

Down The Rabbit Hole

When Alice went down the rabbit hole, she had nary a clue as to what awaited her beyond. An economic measure is no rabbit hole though and the resultant outcomes certainly not unfathomable.

Prime Minister Narendra Modi's historic demonetization announcement on November 8, 2016, was not without precedent even within the Indian context. On January 12, 1946, the Governor-General of pre-Independence Government of India passed the High Denomination Bank Note (Demonetization) Ordinance just after World War II ended. India had its second tryst with demonetization on January 16, 1978, when the Janata Dal Government announced that Rs 1,000, Rs 5,000 and Rs 10,000 notes would be withdrawn from circulation.[7]

So, when Prime Minister Modi made that momentous announcement, he did have the lessons of history to fall back on, in addition to the wisdom

---

[7] The High Denomination Bank Notes (Demonetisation) Act, 1978.

of a core[8] group that is said to have discussed and planned the move during the preceding months.

Clearly then, although kept top secret, the move had been on the anvil for a while. To avid political watchers, the announcement should not have come as the bolt from the blue that it was; at least not its intent. As part of his Mann Ki Baat[9] address in the last week of June, Prime Minister Modi reminded tax defaulters about the September 30 deadline for declaring their undisclosed income under an amnesty scheme in operation and warned[10] of strong penal action if they desisted.

The scheme followed a similar initiative[11] adopted the previous year (2015), under the Undisclosed Foreign Income and Assets Bill, which had kept a window open between July and September of that year for disclosure of income and assets on foreign

---

[8] See 'How A Trusted Bureaucrat Led The Top Secret Demonetisation Project In Two Rooms At Modi's Delhi Residence', December 9, 2016, *Huffington Post*, Reuters, http://www.huffingtonpost.in/2016/12/08/how-a-trusted-bureaucrat-led-the-top-secret-demonetisation-proje/

[9] Mann Ki Baat (Hindi: मन की बात) is an Indian radio programme hosted by Prime Minister Narendra Modi in which he addresses the people of the nation on state owned radio and TV channels.

[10] See 'PM Modi reminds tax defaulters of September 30 deadline', June 27, 2016, *The Indian Express*, Express News Service, http://indianexpress.com/article/india/india-news-india/pm-narendra-modi-mann-ki-baat-black-money-tax-evasion-undisclosed-assets-2877963/

[11] See 'Why the govt's new income declaration schemes are different from the amnesties of earlier times', July 21, 2016, *The Indian Express*, Rajesh M Kayal, http://indianexpress.com/article/explained/black-money-declarants-income-declaration-scheme-dispute-resolution-scheme-amnesty-schemes-pm-modi-2926436/

shores. The Voluntary Disclosure Window had netted Rs 3,770 crores[12] in 2015 and Rs 65,250 crores[13] in 2016. Going by the hint dropped by the Prime Minister in his radio address, the government was bound to up the ante on the black money front and so any step in that direction should not have come as a complete surprise.

Only a trusted group[14] of people appeared to be privy to the decision, planning and implementation of the demonetization process. This despite the massive scale of the task involved, where close to 86 percent of the total currency in value was to be withdrawn from circulation and replaced by valid currency of equal value. The decision and planning were probably kept under wraps to ensure the degree of secrecy that was crucial to the success of the mission.

The Union Minister of State for Finance, Arjun Ram Meghwal, in a statement to the Rajya Sabha, said that there were 17,165 million pieces of 500 rupee notes

---

[12] See 'Indians declare Rs 3,770cr under black money amnesty scheme', October 03, 2015, *Money Control*, Shereen Bhan, http://www.moneycontrol.com/news/cnbc-tv18-comments/indians-declare-rs-3770cr-under-black-money-amnesty-scheme_3383781.html

[13] See 'Rs. 65,250 cr. mopped up via new black money window', November 01, 2016, *The Hindu*, http://www.thehindu.com/news/national/black-money-rs-65250-crore-disclosed-under-income-declaration-scheme-says-arun-jaitley/article9173242.ece

[14] See 'How Modi and team kept demonetisation a closely guarded secret', December 09, 2016, *The Hindu*, Reuters, http://www.thehindu.com/news/national/How-Modi-and-team-kept-demonetisation-a-closely-guarded-secret/article16782821.ece

and 6,858 million pieces of 1,000 rupee notes in circulation as on November 8, 2016, the day that Prime Minister Modi announced that the high denomination notes were being demonetized. As on that date, the total value of the currency[15] in the system, in the form of the specified banking notes (SBNs[16]), was Rs 15.44 lakh crore with Rs 8.58 lakh crore in 500 rupee notes and Rs 6.86 lakh crore in 1,000 rupee notes.

In a bid to assess the scale of the task at hand, it becomes important to look at the capacity of the country's currency printing presses. There are four currency presses in India—one each in Nashik (Maharashtra), Dewas (Madhya Pradesh), Salboni (West Bengal) and Mysuru (Karnataka). The first two are owned by the Central Government through the Security Printing and Minting Corporation of India Ltd. According to information[17] available in the Finance Ministry's Annual Report, 2015-16, the yearly currency printing capacity of these two presses is around 40 percent of the total in the country.

---

[15] See 'Demonetisation: Black money calculations don't add up, Modi government may be in for a shock', December 1, 2016, *First Post,* IANS, http://www.firstpost.com/business/demonetisation-black-money-calculations-dont-add-up-modi-government-may-be-in-for-a-shock-3134338.html

[16] SBN or Specified Banking Notes, in the context of this book, refers to the Rs 1000 and Rs 500 notes that ceased to be legal tender from the midnight of November 8, 2016.

[17] See 'Currency Press Capacity: Around 6 Months Needed To Replenish Rs. 500 Notes', November 17, 2016, *NDTV,* IANS, http://www.ndtv.com/india-news/currency-press-capacity-around-6-months-needed-to-replenish-rs-500-notes-1626660

The Cinderella Notes

The other two presses—in Salboni and Mysuru—are part of the Bharatiya Reserve Bank Note Mudran Pvt. Ltd. (BRBNMPL), a wholly—owned subsidiary of the Reserve Bank of India[18] (RBI). These two, comprising 60 percent of the total capacity, can print 16 billion notes in two shifts per year, according to information available on BRBNMPL's website[19]. All four presses put together can, therefore, print a maximum of around 26.66 billion notes while working on two shifts. If all three shifts were run, as the government subsequently clarified, the four presses would be able to print 40 billion notes a year, irrespective of the denomination.

However, printing was only one part of the task. The time taken to move these currency chests across the length and breadth of the country would also have to be factored in. Given the complexity, the task at hand was humongous and it was always going to be a challenge—a fact that the prime minister underlined in his speech even as he exhorted his countrymen to bear with the 'inconveniences' that might result from the move.

While the weapon of demonetization was primarily unleashed to slay the twin demons of black money and counterfeit currency, the former crippling the country's economy and the latter fuelling cross-border terrorism, it was also the proverbial double edged sword that had the ability to cut both ways.

---

[18] The Reserve Bank of India (RBI) is India's central banking institution.
[19] https://www.brbnmpl.co.in/english/

The Cinderella Notes

The economy would hopefully benefit from this operation aimed at cleansing the financial system and unearthing unaccounted for reserves of cash that should have been otherwise deployed in furthering economic growth, and also in shoring up the country's defences against terrorist attacks. On the flip side, it would cause huge upheaval in the lives of the people, with all their high value notes being declared non-fungible overnight.

Keeping in mind the need of the population for emergency services, the Prime Minister clarified[20] that the demonetized currency would continue to be accepted at select outlets for the next 72 hours[21]. These included, among others, public-sector-owned fuel and gas stations, government hospitals and pharmacies, airline and railway ticketing counters, central and state co-operative stores, and at crematoriums and burial grounds.

The demonetization announcement set off excited chatter on social media with people enthused by what they felt would be a definitive war against the corruption that had plagued the system for too long. The idea of taking the wind out of the sails of the

---

[20] See 'PM's address to the Nation', November 8, 2016, *PMINDIA Website*, Speech,
http://www.pmindia.gov.in/en/news_updates/prime-ministers-address-to-the-nation/?comment=disable

[21] The deadline was extended twice subsequently, finally ending on December 2, 2016. See 'Demonetisation: You can use your old Rs 500 notes at petrol pumps and airline counters only till December 2', December 1, 2016, *The Financial Express*, FE Online,
http://www.financialexpress.com/industry/banking-finance/demonetisation-rbi-cuts-rs-500-notes-validity-to-dec-2-from-dec-15-at-petrol-pumps-and-airline-counters/461044/

'enemy', namely cross border terrorist outfits, also held much appeal.

Quite expectedly, there were also desperate attempts by some to try to dispose of some portion of the accumulated SBNs before midnight. It was reported[22] that jewellers, who had shut shop for the day, had to rush back to open their stores post the announcement, given the huge crowds thronging the gold markets. Even on Wednesday, the day following the demonetization announcement, deals were reportedly struck at up to 50 percent premium for purchases made with the SBNs. This led to the prices[23] of gold and silver surging, what with the demonetization announcement being followed by Donald Trump's victory in the 2016 US Presidential elections. The unusual activity in the gold markets did not go unnoticed and the Income Tax sleuths swung into action by demanding that jewellery stores submit CCTV footage for the night of November 8 as well as details of transactions in the immediate wake of demonetization.

Meanwhile, the national media were busy putting up primetime debates and pundits and politicians spent

---

[22] See 'Currency Demonetisation Spikes Up Gold Prices, Government Eyes Clampdown', November 11, 2016, *India Times*, Bobins Abraham, http://www.indiatimes.com/news/india/currency-demonetisation-spikes-up-gold-prices-government-eyes-clampdown-265293.html
[23] See 'Gold, silver prices surge as reaction to demonetisation and Trump win', November 10, 2016, *Business Standard*, Dilip Kumar Jha, http://www.business-standard.com/article/markets/gold-silver-prices-surge-as-reaction-to-demonetisation-and-trump-win-116110901265_1.html

hours discussing the merits of the move and its likely fallout.

There appeared to be a consensus on the fact that the measure would certainly go some ways in crippling/curbing acts of cross border terrorism/ insurgency that were financed by counterfeit currency. A 2015 study[24] by the Indian Statistical Institute, Kolkata, had revealed that, at any given point in time, the value of fake notes in circulation in the economy stood at around Rs 400 crore.

While an estimated Rs 70 crores[25] worth of counterfeit notes are said to enter the system every year, it has been pointed out that, in recent years, there has been a serious dip in the quantum of fake notes confiscated by the authorities.[26]

The demonetization move was also perceived as a body blow to black marketeers, hawala (informal system of inter-city/state/country money transfer) operators and other money hoarders (like real estate

---

[24] See 'Demonetisation to hit terror financing hard', November 10, 2016, *The Hindu,* Pratheesh,
http://www.thehindu.com/news/national/demonetisation-to-hit-terror-financing-hard/article9325696.ece
[25] See 'Narendra Modi's decision to curb fake currency inflow was a calculated strategy', November 9, 2016, *First Post,* Debobrat Ghose,
http://www.firstpost.com/india/narendra-modis-decision-to-curb-fake-currency-inflow-was-a-calculated-strategy-3096460.html
[26] See 'Recovery of fake notes dipped by 30 per cent between 2013 & 2015: Fake became too 'original' to detect', November 13, 2016, *The Indian Express,* Zeeshan Shaikh,
http://indianexpress.com/article/india/india-news-india/recovery-of-fake-notes-dipped-by-30-per-cent-between-2013-2015-fake-became-too-original-to-detect-4372414/

developers/intermediaries), who were also considered the primary conduits for money laundering.

While people who could declare legitimate sources for their cash would feel encouraged to deposit the SBNs into their bank accounts or exchange them over the counter, those with unaccounted for cash would be backed into a corner. The government announced that deposits over Rs 2.5 lakhs[27] would be subject to scrutiny and if the account holders were unable to offer credible explanations on the source (of income), they would be penalised to the extent of 30 percent tax on the unaccounted income in addition to a penalty of 200 percent of the tax amount.

The move was also described as a political masterstroke by the Prime Minister, who had been attacked by the opposition for not acting decisively on fulfilling his poll promise of a war on black money and corruption. With a single move, he had effectively demonstrated his government's commitment to the issue and sent out a strong signal to the world at large that he meant business. This would also mean that India's stock would go up in the international arena as more investors might now evince confidence in the ease of doing business in India without having to resort to corruption or other malpractices.

---

[27] A **lakh** (/'læk/ or /'laːk/; abbreviated **L**; sometimes written **Lac** or **Lacs**) is a unit in the Indian numbering system equal to one hundred thousand (100,000; scientific notation: 10). Source: https://en.wikipedia.org/wiki/Lakh.

One of the benefits that was hardly touched upon, possibly because it was not the stated objective of the exercise, was that it effectively forced the hand of the parallel economy and brought it into the scope of the formal financial system, even if temporarily.

A study by Ambit Capital Research[28] revealed that India's parallel economy was larger than the overall economic size of countries such as Thailand and Argentina. It was also said to account for close to 80 percent of employment[29] in India. With the demonetization move, the money circulating in the parallel economy would be largely recorded and accounted for as it passed through the banking system.

On the flip side, one of the important charges made by those opposing the demonetization move was that a considerable portion of the black money in the country was sunk into real estate or other asset forms. In effect, the demonetization move was going to do nothing to attack the bulk of the black money reserves. While there is no exact projection for the cash component of the total black money in circulation in the country, an expert on the black economy, former JNU[30] professor Arun Kumar,

---

[28] See 'India's black economy shrinking, pegged at 20% of GDP: Report', June 5, 2016, *The Indian Express*, PTI, http://indianexpress.com/article/business/economy/ambit-capital-black-economy-shrinking-pegged-at-20-per-cent-of-gdp-2835783/
[29] See 'Modi's Demonetisation Move May Have Permanently Damaged India's Informal Sector', November 16, 2016, *The Wire*, Pronab Sen, http://thewire.in/80564/modis-demonetisation-move-may-have-permanently-damaged-indias-informal-sector/
[30] Jawaharal Nehru University.

places it at around Rs 6.5 lakh crores[31] based on his formula of using the same velocity of circulation as in the formal economy.

In a bid to gear up to the mammoth task ahead, banks remained closed for a day following the demonetization announcement. Things were largely peaceful although there was a heightened sense of excitement at what was to come. It proved to be the proverbial calm before the storm.

The events that unfolded on November 10 and in the days that followed punctured to a degree the feeling of euphoria that the demonetization announcement had evoked. People appeared to have underestimated the massive scale of operations and their time consuming nature or possibly their excitement blinded them to the fact.

Serpentine queues were seen in front of banks and post offices from the morning of November 10 and also in front of ATMs from November 11 onwards. Adding to the misery was the fact that most of the ATMs had not been calibrated to accept the new 2,000 rupee notes, which were of a different dimension from the existing currency. This, added to the fact that there appeared to be insufficient supply of the new currency notes, resulted in ATMs being rendered non-functional. The only way to get cash was to go to the bank. No wonder bank staff reeled

---

[31] See 'Queues of pain for tiny gain on black money?', November 21, 2016, *The Times of India*, Subodh Varma, http://timesofindia.indiatimes.com/india/Queues-of-pain-for-tiny-gain-on-black-money/articleshow/55532113.cms

under the pressure, having to work overtime as well in a bid to serve the thronging crowds.

Around 200 million, or close to 15 percent of India's population, reportedly continue to remain excluded from the formal banking network.[32] These people had depended solely on their cash holdings to fuel their monetary transactions; the high denominations of which were rendered non-fungible in the open market. Along with existing account holders, they too joined the queues in front of commercial banks and post offices to have their SBNs exchanged.

Those with bank accounts could, of course, deposit their SBNs into their accounts. Those who did not, had no other choice but to join the queues for over-the-counter exchange. Owing to the sudden huge demand for cash, what with the quantum of transactions quadrupling if not more, the government was forced to impose restrictions both on the exchange and also the withdrawal limits on a daily/weekly basis. They were also hampered by the lack of sufficient newly minted currency to replace the SBNs that were being turned in.

With access being either restricted or denied to their own resources, the public grew restive in places, especially those who felt an acute need for cash

---

[32] This estimate can be considered as the lowest common denominator as others have provided varying estimates of the same. Data on India's informal sector is still rather weak, in my opinion. See 'India goes postal in quest to open bank accounts for the masses', January 07, 2016, *Livemint*, Vrishti Beniwal, http://www.livemint.com/Industry/mJ1bj7eb4K3uVs6ocLW84N/India-goes-postal-in-quest-to-open-bank-accounts-for-the-mas.html

owing to ailments, weddings in the family etc. Media reports came in of unfortunate loss of lives, attributed to delay in access to fungible currency. Apart from the human cost, there were also the economic losses to contend with. With people having to wait in queues for cash to service their day to day needs, there was significant loss of productivity (man hours). Cash strapped rural economies[33] were reportedly put through much hardship and the agricultural and manufacturing sectors were among the worst hit. Commercial establishments reported poor occupancy and entire markets, like the fish markets in West Bengal[34] and the wholesale onion markets in Hyderabad[35], were on the verge of being shut down. There were also reports of daily labourers across the country suffering a huge loss of income with trade slowing down considerably and employers not possessing the requisite cash to pay wages.

---

[33] See 'Rural Economy Collapsing, Farmers In Trouble Because Of Demonetisation, Says BJP MP From Porbandar', November 16, 2016, Huffington Post, Rohini Chatterji,
http://www.huffingtonpost.in/2016/11/15/rural-economy-collapsing-farmers-in-trouble-because-of-demoneti/
[34] See 'Demonetisation cripples fishing industry in Bengal', November 25, 2016, *The Hindu,*
http://www.thehindu.com/news/cities/kolkata/demonetisation-cripples-fishing-industry-in-bengal/article9340809.ece and 'Cash crunch: Howrah wholesale fish market on the verge of closure', November 17, 2016, *Hindustan Times*, Subhendu Maiti,
http://www.hindustantimes.com/kolkata/cash-crunch-howrah-wholesale-fish-market-on-the-verge-of-closure/story-zD3wmksCSIPuSyjXmT6vkO.html
[35] See 'Hyderabad: Onion wholesale market closed due to cash crunch in wake of demonetisation', November 16, 2016, *India Today,* Ashish Pandey and Posted by Ankit Misra,
http://indiatoday.intoday.in/story/hyderabad-onion-wholesale-market-demonetisation-of-500-1000-rupee-notes-cash-crunch/1/811913.html

The Cinderella Notes

While demonetization had enabled the absorbing of the informal economy's cash reserves into the formal financial system, it had also left it bereft of the fuel that had kept it going. The lack of penetration of banking services into remote areas and the grossly over-exaggerated reach of the digital economy were made glaringly obvious. From the initial estimate of a few days, the government revised the time frame for normalcy to be restored to close to two months. The Prime Minister, in a public meeting, appealed to his citizens to give him fifty days to complete the task on hand.[36]

It would seem that the government had somehow underestimated the mammoth scale of the task they had undertaken, with matters further complicated by India's size and the complexity of her terrain. The numbers in the form of statistics had probably not prepared them for the sheer scale of cash transactions in the country and consequently, the overnight demand to have actual physical currency to be replaced. The presence of digital payment gateways, mobile and online banking transactions, had clearly not grown to such a degree where people were able to cope with the lack of physical currency that made up an estimated 86 percent in value of the country's physical cash reserves.

---

[36] See 'Will risk even my life but will not give up the fight against black money: PM Narendra Modi', November 14, 2016, *The Economic Times*, ET Bureau,
http://economictimes.indiatimes.com/news/politics-and-nation/emotional-modi-asks-india-for-50-days-to-streamline-currency-spike/articleshow/55400961.cms

The Cinderella Notes

Although the production of currency notes of Rs 2,000 and Rs 500 denomination had reportedly started two months prior to demonetization of the SBNs,[37] the time frame was evidently not enough to ensure replacement of the entire value of the currency rendered non-fungible. Even while it was reported that the production of currency in smaller denominations like Rs 100 and Rs 50 had been stepped up, there was no clear data on the exact quantum of notes available. According to the RBI's response to an RTI[38] (Right to Information) query, the total value[39] of the newly minted two thousand rupee notes with the RBI at the time of demonetization was Rs 4.94 lakh crores[40].

It must be pointed out here that given the higher denomination (Rs 2,000) of the new currency being introduced, it was imperative that the government

---

[37] See 'Don't hoard currency, sufficient notes in supply: RBI', November 17, 2016, *Deccan Herald,* PTI, http://www.deccanherald.com/content/581579/dont-hoard-currency-sufficient-notes.html

[38] Right to Information (RTI) is an Act of the Parliament of India "to provide for setting out the practical regime of right to information for citizens" and replaces the erstwhile Freedom of information Act, 2002. Under the provisions of the Act, any citizen of India may request information from a "public authority" (a body of Government or "instrumentality of State") which is required to reply expeditiously or within thirty days.

[39] See 'On November 8, RBI had only Rs 4.94 lakh crore in 2000 rupee notes: RTI', December 19, 2016, *The Economic Times,* PTI, http://economictimes.indiatimes.com/news/economy/finance/on-november-8-rbi-had-only-rs-4-94-lakh-crore-in-2000-rupee-notes-rti/articleshow/56065299.cms

[40] A **crore** (/'krɔər/; abbreviated **cr**) denotes ten million (10,000,000 or 10^7 in scientific notation) and is equals to 100 lakhs in the Indian numbering system. Source: https://en.wikipedia.org/wiki/Crore

ensured sufficient supply of smaller denomination notes considering the large number of micro transactions and the consequent need for small change. Also, the recalibration of ATMs ought to have happened well ahead of the demonetization to ensure that they were physically ready to cope with the newly minted currency[41].

There has been much speculation[42] on the seeming lack of preparedness on the part of the government in both these instances. Although a circular was sent out to the banks on recalibrating ATMs, of course citing altogether different reasons and offering incentives, the time-frame provided therein was subsequently abruptly cut short and the demonetization announcement made even before the efforts could be completed. The question arises as to whether some kind of security breach occurred, which forced the government into making the announcement before all preparations were in place. The images of the newly minted Rs 2000 note circulating on social media lends credence to speculation on a leak.

The digital economy suffered breakdowns and glitches even as it struggled to cope with the sudden leap in the quantum of transactions. There were

---

[41] The need to change the size of the currency note is baffling. Retaining the same size would have surely helped in avoiding the need for ATM calibration.

[42] See 'Demonetisation: PM Modi aborted plan to calibrate ATMs for Rs 100 notes. Why?', November 19, 2016, *First Post*, Bindisha Sarang and BV Rao, http://www.firstpost.com/business/demonetisation-pm-modi-aborted-plan-to-calibrate-atms-for-rs-100-notes-why-3112020.html

reports of several instances of failure of debit/credit card machines and even rejection of credit cards of multiple customers with excellent track records and requisite limits. There were also reports of transactions failing subsequent to the TELCOS[43] taking the money due on them from the customer's credit/debit card. It must be clarified at this juncture that glitches in digital transactions are certainly not a new phenomenon that can be attributed solely to demonetization.

While the sheer scale of operations explains a few hiccups here and there, such huge upheavals do make one wonder how things could have possibly been done differently to minimize the 'sufferings' of the common man.

First, such a massive scale operation necessitated a certain military kind of preparedness, something that probably a civilian workforce cannot hope to match. So, would it have served the mission better if the armed forces had been deployed in the management of currency distribution? The Prime Minister had, after all, described it as 'the war against corruption'. The sheer volume of effort required and the possible human crises that could be a fallout of the demonetization exercise probably called for the presence and involvement of the army, particularly in matters like reaching the replacement currency reserves to remote areas on time. In this context, it must be mentioned that IAF[44] aircraft[45] were

---

[43] Telecom companies = TELCOS
[44] The Indian Air Force (IAF; IAST: Bhāratīya Vāyu Senā) is the air arm of the Indian armed forces.

deployed to carry currency at speed across the country, particularly the difficult to access regions.

Second, of course, is the matter of sufficient currency to meet the wholesale demand arising out of demonetization. We have no clear cut data on this and the government has been repeatedly saying that there is no dearth of cash[46] although the huge restrictions on outflow and never ending queues present a contrary picture on the ground. However, large-scale media reports on IT raids[47] unearthing huge caches of newly minted currency lead one to speculate on the extent to which the dearth of cash was a result of malpractice—where black money hoarders possibly colluded with bank authorities to intercept and exchange their reserves, leaving very little for the genuine needs of the common man!

Third, the government did seem a little underprepared when it came to recognizing the special needs of sections of the population, like

---

[45] See 'Indian Air Force's Biggest Aircraft Are Now Ferrying Tonnes Of Currency Across India', November 29, 2016, *The Huffington Post*, Sudhi Ranjan Sen,
http://www.huffingtonpost.in/2016/11/28/indian-air-forces-biggest-aircraft-are-now-ferrying-tonnes-of-c/
[46] See 'Banks have enough cash for exchange of demonetised notes: RBI', November 11, 2016, *Indo-Asian News Service (IANS)*,
http://www.business-standard.com/article/economy-policy/banks-have-enough-cash-for-exchange-of-demonetised-notes-rbi-116111100936_1.html
[47] See 'Even as common man is stuck in bank lines, raids have unearthed Rs 160 crores of new currency notes', December 26, 2016, Scroll.in, Shoaib Daniyal,
http://scroll.in/article/823912/even-as-common-man-is-stuck-in-bank-lines-raids-have-unearthed-rs-160-crores-of-new-currency-notes

farmers and daily wagers among others, and perhaps did not make sufficient allowances for the same.

Fourth, it might have been beneficial if the government had set up a 24 hour helpline that people could access in crisis situations. A support system to reach out in case of medical or other emergencies etc. would have gone some way in mitigating the anguish of the citizens. In this context, it is imperative to point out the reported efforts of the Chief Ministers of states like Maharashtra,[48] Andhra Pradesh,[49] Telangana,[50] and Odisha,[51] who took extra care to reduce the sufferings of the people of their states and the arrangements that were made in this context.

Despite all the stringent precautions, it must be noted that there were reportedly attempts made to exploit loopholes and to launder black money reserves using

---

[48] See 'Currency demonetisation: CM Devendra Fadnavis asks urban local bodies to keep payment counters open today', November 14, 2016, The Indian Express, Express News Service, http://indianexpress.com/article/india/india-news-india/currency-demonetisation-cm-devendra-fadnavis-asks-urban-local-bodies-to-keep-payment-counters-open-today-4373880/

[49] See 'Demonetisation: Why Chandrababu Naidu is the only non-BJP CM to hail move', November 18, 2016, First Post, GS Radhakrishna, http://www.firstpost.com/politics/demonetisation-why-chandrababu-naidu-is-the-only-non-bjp-cm-to-hail-move-3111644.html

[50] See 'Demonetisation: Tokens to ease Kukatpally Rythu Bazaar 'change' woes', November 19, 2016, Deccan Chronicle, http://www.deccanchronicle.com/nation/current-affairs/191116/demonetisation-tokens-to-ease-kukatpally-rythu-bazaar-change-woes.html

[51] See 'Farmers of Odisha go digital', February 15, 2016, Livemint, Harveen Ahluwalia, http://www.livemint.com/Politics/wHiHYViu0X4Q9nsDsZeHlL/Farmers-of-Odisha-go-digital.html

Jan Dhan accounts,[52] specially created to bring the financially excluded into the formal economy. There were also instances of employers using the accounts of poor employees[53] to launder their black money reserves. Various other innovative efforts to beat the demonetization trap[54] came to light as well. Quite obviously, these caught the attention of the authorities, who tried to counter them by restricting over—the—counter currency exchanges[55] and warned of legal action against those who were party to the laundering efforts.[56] It must be stated that in this cat and mouse game between the government and the money launderers, there were frequent

---

[52] See 'Parallel economy: Jan-Dhan accounts used to launder money', November 15, 2016, *The Times of India,* B V Shiva Shankar, http://timesofindia.indiatimes.com/city/bengaluru/Parallel-economy-springsup-Jan-Dhan-accountsused-to-launder-money/articleshow/55423362.cms

[53] See 'Poor people become black money mules for rich', November 13, 2016, *India Today,* Siddhartha Rai and Posted by Anand, Jayaram, http://indiatoday.intoday.in/story/poor-black-money-mules-rich/1/809457.html

[54] See 'The great Indian jugaad: How some are beating the Rs 1,000 note ban', November 11, 2016, *Business Standard,* BS Web Team, http://www.business-standard.com/article/economy-policy/the-great-indian-jugaad-how-some-are-beating-the-rs-1000-note-ban-116111100406_1.html

[55] See 'Modi government applies more curbs, limits bank exchange from Rs 4,500 to Rs 2000', November 17, 2016, *The Economic Times,* Economictimes.Com, http://economictimes.indiatimes.com/news/economy/policy/modi-government-applies-more-curbs-limits-bank-exchange-from-rs-4500-to-rs-2000/articleshow/55470284.cms

[56] See 'Demonetisation: Misuse of bank account for black money deposit to invite govt action', November 24, 2016, *The Indian Express,* PTI, http://indianexpress.com/article/india/india-news-india/demonetisation-government-to-prosecute-jan-dhan-account-holders-for-black-money-deposit-4382373/

changes[57] in rules/ procedures with regard to the banking/exchange of the SBNs. Amidst all the chaos and stories of anguish and suffering, there were a few heart-warming stories of innovation and trust. Like the case of the village that suffered not an iota on account of demonetization because they had already turned cashless[58] or the case of the community that used notes[59] in place of currency. There were also instances where people put up a display of enterprise by resorting to age old barter systems[60] in a bid to beat the cash crunch. There were personally recounted stories of the credit reputation of the small traders coming to their help.

As of December 10, 2016, the total value of SBNs deposited[61] with the RBI stood at Rs 12.44 lakh

---

[57] See '59 demonetisation changes before 50 days: Here are 10 important developments', December 20, 2016, *The Financial Express*, FE Online,
http://www.financialexpress.com/economy/59-demonetisation-changes-before-50-days-here-are-10-important-developments/480212/

[58] See 'Amid banknotes chaos, 'digital' village that turned cashless is an oasis of calm', November 12, 2016, *Hindustan Times*, Hiral Dave,
http://www.hindustantimes.com/india-news/amid-banknotes-chaos-digital-village that-turned-cashless-is-an-oasis-of-calm/story-BRMwBCXMR7MGMiZs8dG8bM.html

[59] See ''Notes' replace notes in Mizoram village', November 16, 2016, *The Times of India*,
http://timesofindia.indiatimes.com/city/guwahati/Notes-replace-notes-in-Mizoram-village/articleshow/55451270.cms

[60] See 'India's jugaad: Modi's demonetisation brings back the ancient barter system', November 15, 2016, Catch News, Sahil Bhalla,
http://www.catchnews.com/india-news/india-s-jugaad-modi-s-demonetisation-brings-back-the-ancient-barter-system-1479148760.html

[61] See 'Shri R. Gandhi and Shri S. S. Mundra, RBI Deputy Governors brief Agencies on Currency Issues: Edited Transcript', December 13,

crores. The value of currency replaced amounted to Rs 4.61 lakh crore. What these figures indicate is that a little over a third of the money that had returned to the system was conveyed back to the public in the form of cash. While these statistics offer a numerical perspective on the demonetization process, the lacunae in the implementation and the consequent losses are the indicators of the degree of process failure.

Realizing the consequences of demonetization on certain sections of the economy in the short run and the growing threat of an economic slowdown, the Indian government tried to mitigate the losses to some extent by relaxing the stringent restrictions originally imposed. There was a relaxation of withdrawal limits for certain categories like farmers, small traders and also special circumstances like weddings subject to certain checks, and farmers[62] were allowed to use the SBNs to purchase seeds from centre or state run and other notified supply outlets. While there was criticism on frequent policy changes, I would compare the implementation of demonetization decision, to some extent, with the tweaking of a war strategy to suit the changing ground situation.

2016, *RBI Press Release,*
https://rbi.org.in/Scripts/BS_PressReleaseDisplay.aspx?prid=38886
[62] See 'Government allows farmers to buy seeds with old Rs 500 notes', November 21, 2016, *The Economic Times,* PTI,
http://economictimes.indiatimes.com/news/economy/agriculture/government-allows-farmers-to-buy-seeds-with-old-rs-500-notes/articleshow/55539367.cms

The Cinderella Notes

Even while acknowledging the negative fallouts of the move, it needs to be strongly emphasized that the demonetization exercise marks a significant step in India's fight against corruption and its bid to mainstream the shadow economy. Without a doubt, Prime Minister Narendra Modi demonstrated tremendous political will in living up to one of his most important poll promises—that of fighting against the corruption which has been eating into the Indian economy for too long. He has also said that demonetization is only a component of the larger strategy against black money and corruption and has hinted at more to come[63].

The jury continues to be out on the efficacy of demonetization as a strategy. Some experts are also sceptical of long standing benefits going by historic precedent. However, we live in digital times today, which afford huge possibilities for the emergence of a largely cashless economy. Given that cash has a direct correlation with corruption and the black markets, a move towards cashless payment systems could surely be a huge step in addressing the issues that plague the Indian economy. There are also the disadvantages to an excessively cash dependent economy that will hopefully be addressed in this process. Also, by merging the parallel economy with the formal economy, a legitimate recognition of the contribution of the informal sector to the GDP can

[63] See 'Demonetisation: 'Emotional' PM Narendra Modi vows, "This is just the beginning, more to come"', November 22, 2016, *The Financial Express*, http://www.financialexpress.com/india-news/demonetisation-pm-narendra-modi-vows-this-is-just-the-beginning-more-to-come/452372/

be achieved and also, the constituents of the informal sector can be afforded the opportunities that a formal financial system has to offer. Mopping up of cash resources from the informal sector will also improve tax yields and offer more capital for public infrastructure building, employment generating initiatives etc. In the light of all this, I am of the considered opinion that it would be premature to write off the benefits of the demonetization move at this stage, given its long-term implications.

Media reports have extensively chronicled the impact of demonetization on the economy and the various process issues related to the implementation. The immediate fallouts of demonetization need to be addressed with a deep sense of urgency and confidence needs to be restored in the minds of the people, urging them to revert to their normal consumption patterns. The losses suffered by the various sectors as a result of the cash crunch and the general fear psychosis that is prompting people to hoard/save are expected to contribute to a slowing down of the economy. There are already predictions of a cut in the growth rate not only by economists but also by rating agencies.[64]

A slew of constructive and forward looking backup measures in several areas/sectors—informal & unorganized sector enterprises, (digital) financial inclusion, real estate, media & entertainment, urban

---

[64] See 'Cash crunch: Analysts cut India GDP growth forecast', November 24, 2016, *Livemint*,
http://www.livemint.com/Politics/gG3pF45hFU53GyXE1BwIuJ/C ash-crunch-Analysts-cut-India-GDP-growth-forecast.html

& rural governance at all levels—are an imperative with a view to jumpstarting and stimulating demand[65] and to counter the projected overall slowing down of the economy. These measures are critical to making the wheels of growth churn and at a rapid pace. Otherwise, India's phenomenal growth story could effectively be over for some time to come.

---

[65] These would also help in ensuring that there is no generation of black money in the system in the future and all monies essentially flow only through the national payments systems and formal channels.

CHAPTER 3

Cracking the Digital Code

Perception is one thing and reality altogether another. This can't be truer than for the reach of digital financial systems in India. With *Paytm*[66] becoming synonymous with payments, much like *Google* with search, it seemed as if the whole country was getting wrapped up in a giant digital bubble. That is, until demonetization became the pinprick that burst it. The stark reality is that cash is what makes the Indian economy go around. In its absence, the wheels of the economy have begun to slowly grind to a halt even as the digital financial systems are creaking under the weight of the quantum leap in the volume of transactions.

India's tryst with digital finance began with the advent of internet banking close to two decades ago, but the true proliferation occurred with the large scale entry of mobile banking services. The country's central banking institution, the Reserve Bank of India (RBI) issued its first set of guidelines[67] on mobile

[66] Paytm is a mobile payment gateway that claims to enjoy an 80% market share.
[67] See 'Mobile Payments in India - Operative Guidelines for Banks', June 12, 2008, *Reserve Bank of India*, Press Release, https://rbidocs.rbi.org.in/rdocs/PressRelease/PDFs/84979.pdf

banking in the year 2008. The e-commerce market has witnessed an exponential growth since then, from $3.8 billion in 2009 to $12.6 billion in 2013[68]. It is expected to touch $15 billion by the end of 2016 with the number of online shoppers touching 100 million.[69]

While the numbers seem independently impressive, a McKinsey Global Insights report reveals that less than 1 percent of the total financial transactions[70] by volume are cashless. As per the Reserve Bank's provisional data[71] for the FY 2015-16, the total value of non-cash transactions in the country stood at Rs 1,835,102.59 billion or approximately $26 trillion. Out of this, digital[72] transactions amounted to Rs 10,175.88 billion or a negligible 0.55 percent. In terms of volume of transactions, digital transactions stood at 21.96 percent of the total non-cash transactions.

---

[68] See 'Evolution of e-commerce in India: Creating the bricks behind the clicks', August 2014, *ASSOCHAM* and *PWC*,
http://www.pwc.in/assets/pdfs/publications/2014/evolution-of-e-commerce-in-india.pdf
[69] See 'Online shoppers in India to cross 100 million by 2016: Study', November 20, 2014, *Gadgets Now*, IANS,
 http://www.gadgetsnow.com/tech-news/Online-shoppers-in-India-to-cross-100-million-by-2016-Study/articleshow/45217773.cms
[70] See 'Is India headed towards becoming a cashless economy?', November 9, 2016, *Governance Now*, Taru Bhatia,
http://www.governancenow.com/news/regular-story/-india-headed-wards-becoming-a-cashless-economy
[71] See 'RBI Bulletin', Nov 10, 2016, *RBI*,
https://rbi.org.in/scripts/BS_ViewBulletin.aspx?Id=16609
[72] For the computation of value of digital transactions, we have included Credit card (POS), Debit Card (POS) and Mobile payments.

The Cinderella Notes

The significance of all these numbers was brought home by the events that followed demonetization Banks suddenly found themselves having to service not only their own clientele but also those who had hitherto remained unbanked. It was this fact that translated into the scenario of serpentine queues in front of the banks and ATMs in the days that followed demonetization. People who had never seen the inside of a bank, and those who had chosen not to engage significantly with the formal financial system queued up outside the formal institutions because demonetization had rendered a significant portion of their currency non-fungible.

Statistics on the penetration of banking services across the country will help gain insight into the enormity of the decision and the massive scale of operations that it entailed.

As of March 2015, India had a total of 102,343 bank branches, including nationalised, private, foreign and regional rural banks, while the total number of ATMs stood at 218,542 as of September, 2016. Only 38 percent[73] of the branches of the scheduled commercial banks were in rural areas. Of the ATMs, only 19 percent were located in rural areas, home to about 70 percent of the Indian population.

With the delay in calibrating the ATMs to handle the new currency, the hundred thousand plus bank

---

[73] See 'Bharat has 70% of population, but only 19% of ATMs', November 28, 2016, *Business Standard*, Ishan Bakshi, http://www.rediff.com/business/report/note-scrapping-19-of-atms-for-70-of-population/20161128.htm

branches were left to cope with the demand from all of India that needed to deposit/exchange the SBNs in its possession. Of course, close to 150,000 post offices[74] were also pressed into service. And yet, the sheer volume of transactions was such that the system was left red faced and coming apart at the seams, thanks to the overnight run on its capacity.

The lead time per customer also increased significantly, not only because of additional processes like checking identity cards and collecting their photocopies, but also in having to deal with a fresh subset of the population that did not possess much by way of financial or process literacy. As if these challenges were not enough, there was also the shortage of fresh currency notes to deal with.

With the physical banking resources reeling under the sudden quantum leap in transactions, it was time for the digital financial sector to step in. However, their client base was not massive enough for them to make a serious dent, as a result of which, a majority of India was still left waiting outside banks.

A look at three pieces of statistics will help explain some of the challenges that the digital financial system needs to negotiate in the process of trying to maximise its reach across the country. The first is that only 53 percent of the adult population has bank accounts and even those suffer a very high dormancy rate. Second, just 39 percent of all account holders in

---

[74] See 'Post Offices (1947-2016)' *Indiastat,*
http://www.indiastat.com/telecommunication/28/post/218/postoff
ices19472016/449519/stats.aspx

India are said to own a debit or ATM card. Third, only 1.4 million POS (point of sale) terminals exist across the country, primarily in urban centres.[75]

With bank accounts a necessary prerequisite to most digital payment solutions, close to half of India's adult population gets excluded right up front. Effective use of technology demands a certain level of literacy and dexterity. Besides, there are the impediments in the form of access to uninterrupted mobile data networks and the availability of infrastructure to support the digital way of transacting.

Apart from the issues on the ground that are obstacles to increased penetration of digital services, one needs to consider that, as a people, Indians are cash-obsessed. They like the idea of physical cash in their hands and the sense of security that it offers them. India is, after all, among the most cash intensive economies in the world.

Only[76] about 11 per cent households in urban areas and 0.43 percent per cent households in rural India make cashless transactions.

---

[75] See 'Demonetisation Isn't an 'Inconvenience', It's a Gross Violation of Our Rights', November 20, 2016, *The Wire,* Rashmi Venkatesan, http://thewire.in/81364/demonetisation-rights-violation/

[76] See 'Only 3.6% households go in for cashless dealings: Report', September 6, 2013, *The Times of India,* PTI, http://timesofindia.indiatimes.com/business/india-business/Only-3-6-households-go-in-for-cashless-dealings-Report/articleshow/22370847.cms

As per a Deutsche bank report, currency as a percentage of GDP stood at 12.2 percent.[77] This gives India the dubious distinction of having the highest currency to GDP ratio[78], among emerging economies. Yet another metric measure of cash intensity is the monetary aggregate (M0/M2).[79] In the case of India, the monetary aggregate, i.e., M0 as a ratio of M2, is greater than 50 percent. Here, it needs to be emphasized that this value of monetary aggregate is again higher in comparison to that of other emerging economies such as Mexico (9 percent), South Africa (9 percent), and China (5 percent). Furthermore, even in a highly cash-intensive country such as Egypt, M0 is just 24 percent of M2. And when worldwide data is considered, what emerges is the salient fact that India has the highest share of cash transactions across developed, emerging and developing countries.[80]

A cash economy comes at a steep cost as expenses are incurred on physical currency production and

---

[77] See 'India one of the most cash intensive economies', November 15, 2016, *Livemint*,
http://www.livemint.com/Money/CVkOV1emoQwCNXh0TZPyK I/India-one-of-the-most-cash-intensive-economies.html
[78] See 'India's currency-GDP ratio highest among BRICS nations', November 23, 2016, *The Times of India*, M.Allirajan
http://timesofindia.indiatimes.com/business/india-business/Indias-currency-GDP-ratio-highest-among-BRICS-nations/articleshow/55576351.cms
[79] M0 is the amount of money held in bills and coins and M2 is the amount held in demand deposit and savings accounts. M0/M2 is a very good indicator of cash intensity.
[80] See 'E-payments: Revolutionary transformation in the Indian payment system', December 28 - Jan 01, 2016, *ICICI Securities*,
http://content.icicidirect.com/mailimages/Payments.htm

distribution, apart from the transaction costs involved in handling them. The Reserve Bank of India (RBI) and the commercial banks spend about Rs 21,000 crore ($3.5 billion) annually to print as well as circulate currency notes and coins, and thereafter keep them safe.[81] The significance of the lead time associated with both production and distribution has been sharply underscored now, especially because of the severe cash crunch that banks have faced post demonetization. Additionally, the degree of hardship that people in rural and remote areas have suffered as a consequence of the currency not reaching them quickly is another factor to consider here.

Even while acknowledging the demerits of a cash intensive economy, it is important to take a look at the issue from the other end of the equation. The most straightforward point in favour of cash as currency is seigniorage. In simple terms, seigniorage is the difference or the profit earned by the government on issuance of currency, the value being the difference between the cost of production and the face value of the currency. If the seigniorage is positive, then the government will make an economic profit; a negative seigniorage will result in an economic loss. Seigniorage gives a country the potential to turn a profit when money is produced. However, in the shift to a cashless economy, the government runs the risk of losing out its seigniorage privileges. If the phase-out of paper currency were

---

[81] 'Is India headed towards becoming a cashless economy?', November 9, 2016, *Governance now*, Taru Bhatia, http://www.governancenow.com/news/regular-story/-india-headed-wards-becoming-a-cashless-economy

simply met by an increased demand for electronic central bank reserves, there would, of course, be no significant loss. On the flip side, since paper currency is anonymous, replacing it with non-anonymous electronic money may well lead to a large shrinkage in demand, and the Government Treasury would have to absorb the loss. This cost might be somewhat compensated if a modest fraction of the underground economy is induced to pay taxes, and there are gains to be had from reduced costs of monitoring and enforcement.

There is also a question of how forcing a more rapid shift to cashless payments would affect transaction costs for businesses. Retailers are typically forced to pay a pro-rata fee to companies such as MasterCard and Visa for credit card services. Furthermore, handling paper currency also entails substantial costs to protect it against theft and pilferage.

The Harvard economist Kenneth Rogoff,[82] in an academic paper, plays the devil's advocate as he discusses the various points in favour of maintaining paper currency, including the need to maintain a diversity of technologies, the issue of civil liberties that pertain to a government's access to and control of personal financial data, the risk of foreign currency coming into usage, the durability of cash as currency despite the various technological advancements and so on. However, given the role of paper currency (especially large-denomination notes) in facilitating

---

[82] See 'Costs and benefits to phasing out paper currency', April 11, 2014, *Presented at NBER Macroeconomics Annual Conference*, Kenneth Rogoff, http://scholar.harvard.edu/files/rogoff/files/c13431.pdf

tax evasion and illegal activity, and the perpetuation of a parallel economy, he does point out that a gradual phasing out of paper currency would be beneficial to the economy.

Coming back to the present (Indian) context, the first pre-requisite for an effective digital financial system would be a widespread banking network with excellent ground coverage. Digital payment wallets are most often linked to the commercial bank accounts or the credit cards of customers. The country has among the poorest of ratios in terms of the population expected to be serviced by a single bank branch with RBI data placing it at around 10 bank branches and 14 ATMs per 100,000 as of the year 2015.[83] While there is a more even distribution of the bank branches across the country, the ATMs are concentrated in the metropolitan cities.

In this context, Prime Minister Narendra Modi's government launched a flagship programme, Pradhan Mantri Jan-Dhan Yojana (PMJDY) that deserves mention. It was primarily aimed at enabling the inclusion of those excluded from the formal financial system. 24.2 crore new banks accounts have been opened under this scheme since its launch in 2014, both in rural and urban areas. The Jan Dhan accounts[84] have been linked to the Aadhar[85] cards

---

[83] See 'E-payments: Revolutionary transformation in the Indian payment system', December 28 - Jan 01, 2016, *ICICI Securities*, http://content.icicidirect.com/mailimages/Payments.htm

[84] See 'India has started linking Jan Dhan scheme, Aadhaar and mobile numbers: Arun Jaitley', April 02, 2016, *Livemint*, Asit Ranjan Mishra,

and, wherever possible, the mobile numbers of the account holders so cash subsidies for the poor and the marginalized may be routed through these accounts. This strategy has been adopted to encourage the excluded population to be a part of the formal financial system. The innovative JAM (short for Jan Dhan-Aadhaar-Mobile) trinity was first proposed in the Economic Survey 2014-15. As of April 2016, the PMJDY[86] accounts held a sum total of Rs 37,617 crore as balance or about Rs 1,700 per account. Each of these account holders has been issued a debit card apart from enjoying an overdraft facility of up to Rs 5000. Kisan credit cards are also issued to farmers to help finance their short term production credit needs in a simple and hassle free manner.

Over the years, various studies have documented how countries could benefit by moving from cash to digital payments. According to a 2016 Moody's Analytics study, USD 296 billion has reportedly been added to global consumption by card usage—this translates to a cumulative 0.1 percentage increase in global GDP. Furthermore, this is also reported to

---

http://www.livemint.com/Politics/PRmacll IkzL6fCJEUIVLo3H/I ndia-has-started-linking-Jan-Dhan-scheme-Aadhaar-and-mobil.html

[85] Aadhaar is a 12-digit unique identification number issued by the Indian government to every individual resident of India. The Unique Identification Authority of India (UDAI), which functions under the Planning Commission of India, is responsible for managing Aadhaar numbers and Aadhaar identification cards.

[86] See 'Jan Dhan scorecard: 22 cr bank accounts opened, average balance Rs 1,725', May 26, 2016, *The Times of India*, Subodh Varma, http://timesofindia.indiatimes.com/india/Jan-Dhan-scorecard-22-cr-bank-accounts-opened-average-balance-Rs-1725/articleshow/52442488.cms

have created around 13 million jobs during the period 2011 to 2015.[87]

A Reserve Bank of India (RBI) report released in March, 2016, titled *Concept Paper on Card Acceptance Infrastructure*[88], placed India's average number of card transactions per inhabitant at 6.7, which is among the lowest in the world. It is 249.3 in Australia, 247.9 in Canada, 201.7 in the UK, 54.8 in Brazil and 14.4 in China.

As of December, 2015, 22.74 million credit cards were in use in India, while the number of debit cards stood at 636.85 million. The above RBI report places usage of debit cards at ATMs at 88 percent of the total volume and at around 94 percent of the total value of debit card transactions. Compared to this, transactions at point of sale (PoS) terminals account for only 12 percent of volume and 6 percent of the value of transactions.

As per a JM Financial report, *Card penetration in India,*[89] the number of PoS devices stood at 1.2

---

[87] See 'Accelerating The Growth of Digital Payments in India: A Five - Year Outlook', October, 2016, *VISA,*
http://www.visa.co.in/aboutvisa/research/include/Digital_Payment s_India.pdf
[88] See' Concept Paper on Card Acceptance Infrastructure', April 15, 2016, *Department of Payment and Settlement Systems,* Reserve Bank of India,
https://rbidocs.rbi.org.in/rdocs/PublicationReport/Pdfs/MDRDB EDA36AB77C4C81A3951C4679DAE68F.PDF
[89] See 'Why cash is still king for Indian consumers', April 20 2016, *Livemint,* Tania Kishore Jaleel,
http://www.livemint.com/Money/jCjgdI36iBHWt30hN3gOSP/Wh y-cash-is-still-king-for-Indian-consumers.html

million for over 14 million estimated merchants, which translates to almost 90 percent of the outlets being left without a mechanism to collect payments electronically. The report also pointed out that while almost every bank was a diligent card issuer, few were engaged in the task of merchant acquisition and setting up of the acceptance infrastructure.

Yet another point needs emphasis here. Point-of-sale (POS) terminals in India cost between INR 8,000 (USD 118.9) to INR 12,000 (USD 178.3). It is important to note that countervailing duties and taxes account for about 20 percent of the price. Furthermore, the yearly operating cost[90] ranges from INR 3,000 (USD 44.6) to INR 4,000 (USD 59.40) for one terminal.[91] The high costs of acquisition and maintenance of POS terminals make it unviable for small merchants and those in rural areas to invest in them, given the low value and volume of transactions. This, in turn, can be attributed to the lack of penetration of banking/financial services and uninterrupted/poor connectivity.

There is also a significant gender divide when it comes to the adoption of financial services in general

---

[90] This is said to include paper and servicing costs, totalling about INR 3.9 billion (USD 60 million) on a yearly basis for all installed 1.3 million terminals. See 'Accelerating The Growth of Digital Payments in India: A Five-Year Outlook', October, 2016, *VISA*, http://www.visa.co.in/aboutvisa/research/include/Digital_Payments_India.pdf

[91] See 'Accelerating The Growth of Digital Payments in India: A Five-Year Outlook', October, 2016, *VISA*, http://www.visa.co.in/aboutvisa/research/include/Digital_Payments_India.pdf

and of the digital kind in particular. The fact that women are marginalized both at the workplace and also at home, particularly in the context of financial decision making, has led to this lopsided situation. According to a 2014 World Bank survey,[92] reportedly just 0.38 percent of the women over the age of 15 years used the internet to make payments as compared with about 2.04 percent of men. Likewise, the same survey noted that while 5.25 percent of men had used a debit card, just 3.25 percent of women had done so.

Regulatory limitations impose yet another deterrent to the widespread acceptance of digital financial systems. In September, 2012, the Reserve Bank of India introduced a cap on the merchant discount rate (MDR) on debit card transactions. This reduced the MDR in the market by 50 percent and caused the interchange fees paid to the issuing bank to be reduced correspondingly. The MDR was capped at an ad-valorem rate of 0.75 percent for debit card transactions below INR 2,000 and 1 percent for transactions above INR 2,000. Although the RBI envisaged that this cap would increase the acceptance infrastructure and grow debit card transactions and usage exponentially by reducing cost, this has, unfortunately, not been the case.

All these issues notwithstanding, a move towards digital financial systems is both inevitable and beneficial. An RBI estimate claims that the volume of transactions via mobile banking has doubled between

---

[92] World Bank Financial Inclusion Database, 2014.

2014-15 and 2015-16, going up from 171.92 million to 390 million.[93] Likewise, transactions (by volume) through mobile wallets have also more than doubled during the same period, reaching 604 million in 2015-16 from 255 million in 2014-15. Furthermore, it has been said that this explosion could see total digital finance turnover figures exceeding a whopping $700 billion, registering an 11.8 percent increase by 2025. The resultant increase in GDP is also expected to generate about 21 million jobs in India and make available new loans worth $689 billion to individuals and small businesses. According to a McKinsey Global Insights Report[94], if emerging economies embrace digital finance at such a large scale, it could boost their GDP by as much as six percent.

A recent study by Assocham[95]-RNCOS[96] called 'Indian M-Wallet Market: Forecast 2022' projects the mobile wallet industry[97] to grow from a mere Rs 154 crore in the current fiscal year to as huge as Rs

---

[93] See 'Is India headed towards becoming a cashless economy?', November 9, 2016, *Governance now,* Taru Bhatia, http://www.governancenow.com/news/regular-story/-india-headed-wards-becoming-a-cashless-economy

[94] See 'Is India headed towards becoming a cashless economy?', November 9, 2016, *Governance Now*, Taru Bhatia http://www.governancenow.com/news/regular-story/-india-headed-wards-becoming-a-cashless-economy

[95] This stands for the Associated Chambers of Commerce of India.

[96] RNCOS is a Business Consulting Service firm providing multiple services to companies wishing to engage in any business expansion.

[97] See 'Demonetisation: Why the challenge to take digital payment to rural India is as huge as the opportunity', November 27, 2016, *The Economic Times*, Rajiv Singh, http://economictimes.indiatimes.com/news/economy/policy/sunday-et-making-rural-india-pay-digitally-and-challenges-post-demonetisation/articleshow/55640316.cms

30,000 crore by the year 2022. In terms of value, mobile wallet transactions are expected to increase from Rs 20,600 crore to about Rs 55 lakh crore during the same time period. A global research firm, E-Marketer, likewise projected that, globally, India would become the second largest smartphone market[98] by 2016—with over 200 million active smartphone users—even surpassing the United States. In this context, it should be noted that in the first quarter of 2016, India's smartphone market grew by a huge 23 percent as opposed to a flat annual growth rate globally.[99]

Theoretically, this means that 15-20 percent of the Indian population enjoys potential access to digital financial services in the form of mobile banking apps and mobile wallets. Whether this number translates into active users is moot though, much like whether the 600 million plus debit cardholders, including the 200 million Jan Dhan account holders who were issued RuPay cards, are able to actively use them for their day-to-day monetary transactions.

Despite the overall encouraging projections, there need to be concerted efforts and strategies for both the economy and the end users to derive true benefits from the shift to a digital economy. An RBI

---

[98] See 'India to overtake US in smartphones by 2016', *India in Business*, Indo-Asian News Service,
http://indiainbusiness.nic.in/newdesign/index.php?param=newsdetail/10367
[99] See 'India Smartphone Market Grew 23% Amid Flat Global Annual Growth', April 29, 2016, *Counterpoint Technology Market Research*, Tarun Pathak,
http://www.counterpointresearch.com/india1q16/

report[100] even outlined strategies that need to be put in place to increase the usage of digital systems in financial transactions.

A supportive ecosystem is perhaps the most crucial element for a successful transition to a digital economy. What this means is that mere setting or achieving of targets in terms of outreach is not quite the means to judge the extent of coverage. It needs to be accompanied by an enabling environment and the required infrastructure on the ground. Of what use are debit/credit cards where merchants do not have the required infrastructure to support digital transactions? Conversely, the merchants cannot be expected to invest in infrastructure if it does not prove viable either in terms of value or volume of digital transactions over any given period of time.

Another critical factor is the availability of data network coverage. The level of penetration that mobile wallets can achieve is directly proportional to the ease of data connectivity in an area. An assured supply of quality and uninterrupted connectivity is a crucial component of a successful digital financial ecosystem. Statistics show that of the total number of wireless[101] subscribers in India, a little less than 590 million live in urban areas while about 445 million are

---

[100] See 'RBI Seeks Feedback on Concept Paper on Card Acceptance Infrastructure', March 08, 2016, *Reserve Bank of India,* Press Release, https://www.rbi.org.in/Scripts/BS_PressReleaseDisplay.aspx?prid= 36427

[101] See 'Bharat has 70% of population, but only 19% of ATMs', November 28, 2016, *Business Standard,* Ishan Bakshi, http://www.rediff.com/business/report/note-scrapping-19-of-atms-for-70-of-population/20161128.htm

in rural areas. Similarly, only 230 million in urban areas and 111 million in rural areas have internet access—relatively small numbers.

Yet another important factor that needs to be considered is the process and digital literacy levels of the target population. Unless there is a grasp of the processes involved, be it in terms of financial transactions or the usage of digital payment gateways like mobile banking apps and mobile wallets, it would be extremely difficult for large sections of the population to enter the digital fold.

The issue of data security or safety is most critical too. While digital financial transactions are said to safeguard against the threat of loss that cash exposes people to, given its susceptibility to theft, compromised data safety can also lead to financial losses. We are already familiar with the technique of phishing[102] that reportedly caused Indian businesses to lose close to $4 billion[103] in 2013 alone. Most recently, in October, 2016, there were reports of 3.2 million debits cards being compromised, one of the largest ever breaches[104] of financial data in India. If

---

[102] This is the fraudulent practice of sending emails purporting to be from reputable companies in order to induce individuals to reveal their personal information, such as passwords and credit card numbers, online.

[103] See 'Indian Businesses Lost $4 Billion Due to Cyberattacks in 2013; 2014 to be Worse', December 19, 2014, *Quick Heal Blog*, Rajib Singha, http://blogs.quickheal.com/indian-businesses-lost-4-billion-due-cyberattacks-2013-2014-worse/

[104] See '3.2 million debit cards compromised; SBI, HDFC Bank, ICICI, YES Bank and Axis worst hit', October 20, 2016,*The Economic Times*, Saloni Shukla & Pratik Bhakta, http://economictimes.indiatimes.com/industry/banking/finance/ba

there is to be a large scale shift to digital financial solutions across the country, then it becomes imperative that sufficient checks and balances are put in place to ensure data security.

In the wake of demonetization, digital solutions including debit cards, mobile banking and mobile payment gateways have worked hard to ease the huge strain on the economy, resulting from the cash crunch. According to the Chairman of the NPCI (National Payments Commission of India), there has been a 100 percent[105] increase in digital transactions post demonetization. The number of transactions on the RuPay[106] Card has gone up from 4 lakhs to 10 lakhs[107] per day and Point-of-Sale transactions[108] by 300 percent in volume and 200 percent by value since demonetization. Mobile wallet company transactions have multiplied manifold and there has been a

---

nking/3-2-million-debit-cards-compromised-sbi-hdfc-bank-icici-yes-bank-and-axis-worst-hit/articleshow/54945561.cms

[105] See 'Digital Transactions Up By 100% Since Demonetisation, Says NPCI CEO', November 27, 2016, *The Wire,* Gaurav Vivek Bhatnagar, http://thewire.in/82872/digital-transactions-up-by-100-since-demonetisation-says-ncpi-ceo/

[106] RuPay Card is an Indian version of credit/debit card. It is very similar to international cards such as Visa/Master. National Payments Corporation of India (NPCI) initiated the launch of RuPay card in India. It was done with the intention of integration of payment systems in the country.

[107] See 'RuPay card transactions jump from four lakh/day to 10 lakh', November 22, 2016, *The Hindu Business Line,* G Naga Sridhar, http://www.thehindubusinessline.com/money-and-banking/rupay-card-transactions-jump-from-four-lakhday-to-10-lakh/article9374656.ece

[108] See 'SBI to finish ATM recalibration soon', November 24, 2016, *The Hindu,* M. Soundariya Preetha, http://www.thehindu.com/business/Industry/SBI-to-finish-ATM-recalibration-soon/article16695634.ece

surge[109] in the customer base of digital financial providers companies with some of them recording an increase as high as 150 percent. The government also reached out to digital payment gateway companies to partner in their efforts to help rural India embrace technology as a means of conducting banking and financial transactions.[110] Prime Minister Narendra Modi repeatedly appealed to the citizens to use their mobile phones to conduct banking transactions.[111] With bank accounts increasingly becoming KYC (Know your Customer) compliant with customers' mobile numbers appended to them and also linked to the Aadhar cards of the account holders like in the case of Jan Dhan accounts, mobile banking and mobile wallet transactions become viable alternatives as payment gateways.

In a country with as far flung and complex a terrain as India, the increased provision of physical infrastructure on the ground will always remain a challenge. And, in the wake of a crisis situation that requires swift and precise efforts, conventional strategies alone cannot be relied upon. Even while

---

[109] See 'E-wallet firms' customer base surges', November 25, 2016, *The Hindu,* Lalatendu Mishra,
http://www.thehindu.com/business/E-wallet-firms%E2%80%99-customer-base-surges/article16695644.ece

[110] See 'Government asks Paytm, Oxigen wallet to digitise rural cash', November 21, 2016, *The Economic Times,* Ruchika Chitravanshi,
http://economictimes.indiatimes.com/news/economy/finance/government-asks-paytm-oxigen-wallet-to-digitise-rural-cash/articleshow/55531592.cms

[111] See 'PM Modi pushes for use of mobiles to deal with cash crunch', November 25, 2016, *The Times of India,* PTI,
http://timesofindia.indiatimes.com/india/PM-Modi-pushes-for-use-of-mobiles-to-deal-with-cash-crunch/articleshow/55618832.cms

struggling to cater to the need of physical currency to replace the SBNs, the government strategy has been one of turning a crisis into an opportunity to push the agenda of a relatively cashless economy. It tied in with one of the unsaid objectives of demonetization, integrating the parallel economy with the mainstream.

However, it needs to be reiterated here that, given India's unique challenges in the context of diversity of languages and culture, it might prove counter-productive if the digital payment options are not designed for easy adoption and usage by a heterogeneous population with varying levels of literacy and exposure. Currently, most of the mobile banking solutions as well as the mobile wallets are designed for use by an urban population that is reasonably literate. Wherever vernacular screens are available, the language construct is complex and somewhat beyond the comprehension levels of a not-so-literate set of people with low levels of exposure to digital technology. This level of complexity, be it in design or in language, effectively makes it extremely difficult for the masses to embrace digital financial systems with the kind of alacrity that the establishment expects of them.

In essence, unless processes are simplified all round, it would be very difficult for large sections of the population to actively embrace digital banking solutions in the place of cash transactions that offer the ease of familiarity and simplicity. In the context of simplifying the digital process, it would be important to draw lessons from experiences like that of the Gujarat village[112] that managed to ride the demonetization wave with ease thanks to the adoption of digital payment methods.

It might benefit banks to deploy existing resources like the banking correspondents (with adequate safety)[113] on the ground in enabling people to better negotiate the digital switch. These banking correspondents may be used to spread awareness on digital payment gateways, facilitate their installation on customer mobiles and initially handhold them while they traverse unfamiliar digital terrain. The banking correspondents may be adequately compensated for their services so that they feel encouraged to act as ambassadors of the digital financial ecosystem. Taking into cognizance the existing barriers and challenges that discourage people from embracing the use of digital financial systems, a few creative, user- friendly solutions have been proposed in detail in the Appendix.[114]

The USSD (Unstructured Supplementary Service Data) system that connects almost all major banks in the country does transcend barriers like network connectivity since it is SMS driven. India has over a billion mobile phone users[115] (basic and

---

[112] See 'No cash, no worries for this 'digital' village', November 24, 2016, *The Hindu Business Line*, Virendra Pandit,
http://www.thehindubusinessline.com/news/national/demonetisati
on-no-cash-no-worries-for-this-digital-village/article9381737.ece
[113] Internal control mechanisms for banking correspondents deserves close attention as do internal audits of their operational processes.
[114] See appendix 2.
[115] See 'Indian Telecom Stats: 1 Billion Mobile Subscriber Base Reached, Active Base Cross 902M', January 5, 2016, *Trak.in*, Editorial

smartphones) with the teledensity at 81.18 as of July, 2016.[116] Of course, it must be noted that while the teledensity is a whopping[117] 147.12 in urban areas, it stands at just about halfway mark (51.27) in rural areas.

If concerted efforts are made to help people negotiate process and digital literacy barriers, and an enabling ecosystem is created for the use of digital financial solutions, a fair degree of success can be achieved in encouraging people to make the digital switch. However, apart from all these enabling mechanisms, it is important to encourage people to adopt a new technology at the cost of giving up an exchange system—based on cash—that has served them well for years. They need to be convinced that the new technology is a safe, secure and beneficial means of transacting, bereft of the risks associated with carrying cash around.

The user experience also needs to be made glitch-free. In this context, it must be made clear that digital financial service providers need to up the ante and substantially improve the quality of their service. Demonetization will bring a huge volume of business their way, both in terms of the number of customers as well as transactions, but the opportunity is not

---

Staff, http://trak.in/tags/business/2016/01/05/indian-telecom-stats-1billion-mobile-subscriber-base/

[116] See 'Telecom Regulatory Authority Of India (TRAI)', July 29, 2016, Press Release No. 74/2016, Information Note to the Press, http://www.trai.gov.in/WriteReadData/PressRealease/Document/Press_Release_No74_Eng_29_july_2016.pdf

[117]People using multiple phones could be the reason for this unbelievably huge number.

without its challenges. Their infrastructure and human resources need to gear up to handle the quantum leap in the volume of business.

In the immediate wake of demonetization, one was able to observe a significant increase in glitches/ malfunctions while transacting within the digital space. POS devices are unable to cope with increased volumes of transactions, credit cards of customers with impeccable records are being turned down and there have been too many instances of transactions failing even after the customer accounts have been debited for the value of the transaction. The billing on credit cards does not stand up to scrutiny on several occasions and customers are forced to seek the assistance of helplines to have discrepancies addressed. One would prefer to attribute these discrepancies to process failures rather than any malafide intent. However, a semi-literate or illiterate user would not possess the wherewithal to make note of discrepancies or ensure their rectification. It would be highly unfair on that population if the digital service provider's end up making them pay for what are actually lacunae in the services.

There is also the issue of transaction charges associated with mobile wallets and debit/credit cards. While transaction charges on debit cards[118] have been suspended till December 31, 2016 to enable

---

[118] See 'Latest on demonetisation: No debit card charges and other developments', November 23, 2016, *The Tribune*, PTI, http://www.tribuneindia.com/news/nation/latest-on-demonetisation-debit-card-charges-dropped-and-other-relaxations/327296.html

people to cope with the sudden cash crunch arising out of demonetization, the mobile wallet companies[119] have temporarily dropped the fees they charge their merchants to encourage the use of their service during this phase. However, in the long run, these charges will have to be rationalized. Furthermore, the service providers must pass on some of the huge benefits they will earn—thanks to the manifold increase in the volume of transactions—to their customers in the form of reduced charges. Also, the issue of high and often usurious rates of interest[120] charged on credit card outstanding amounts need to be addressed if the customers are to feel encouraged to avail themselves of the credit facilities these cards offer.

After being blindsided by demonetization, more and more Indians are making the switch to digital payment systems. It is not a voluntary act though; more a kneejerk response to a stimulus. If this needs to be converted into a culture, an enabling environment is critical. The already outlined issues like infrastructure, data connectivity, digital and process literacy, data security and improved service quality need to be addressed on a war footing. The stick has been wielded. It is now time for the carrots to be brought out in the form of incentives and large scale benefits if people are to buy into the idea of a

---

[119] See 'After demonetisation, e-wallets strike it rich while India runs out of cash', November 23, 2016, India Today, Javed Anwer, http://indiatoday.intoday.in/technology/story/after-demonetisation-e-wallets-strike-it-rich-while-india-runs-out-of-cash/1/817932.html
[120] The net effective rate of interest ranges from 36% to 42%, which is usurious by any standard.

cashless digital economy. Now that expediency has forced them to enter the digital fold, it is time to make the experience so worth their while that the love affair turns mutual rather than remain one-sided!

CHAPTER 4

The Realty Show

The best investment on earth is earth
Louis Glickman

Real estate is considered the best and safest of all investment options known to man. While cash or gold run the risk of thievery, investments like stocks and shares are subject to violent market fluctuations and yet others like livestock or any other kind of perishables cannot stand the test of perpetuity. In comparison, real estate is considered the most solid of investments given its perpetual quality, likely incremental value and the marginal chances of loss by theft. While it is also subject to and likely to be impacted by the vagaries of the market, it is nowhere near as volatile, for example, as stocks/shares.

It is these very qualities of real estate that make it so sought after and even fought over. History is replete with instances of wars fought over territory or land and in the modern day context too, there are enough instances of courtroom battles over rights to property. The English philosopher John Locke described the right to property as an inalienable right and said that it was the duty of the state to secure this right for the individual.

Just as it is the world over, the desire to own property is a significant driving force for the majority of the Indian population; a piece of land or a heap of bricks that he can call his own. In the pre-independence era, the Zamindars,[121] the landowners, wielded great political and economic power over the peasantry who tilled their land. With the freedom movement gaining ground in the country, there was opposition to the oppression of the Zamindars and the concentration of power and wealth in the hands of a few. One of the first agrarian reforms immediately after independence was the abolition of the Zamindari system through legislation enacted by the various Indian provinces. However, the Indian Constitution, which came into effect on January 26, 1950, held the right to property as a fundamental right under Articles 19 and 31. With this, all the previous legislations enacted by the provinces on the Zamindari system were rendered constitutionally invalid. It took the first constitutional amendment in 1951 to validate the state acts and by 1956, the Zamindari system had finally been abolished in many Indian provinces.

Although abolished in a legal sense, the degree of power and social status that land ownership invests in an individual cannot be wished away even today.

---

[121] A zamindar in the Indian subcontinent was an aristocrat, typically hereditary, holding enormous tracts of land, and held control over his peasants, from whom the zamindars reserved the right to collect tax often for military purposes.

Hence, a deeply entrenched desire to own property remains with every individual and it is their most prized possession.

Just as their fascination for the yellow metal makes Indians the world's largest consumers of gold[122], the significant influence that the real estate sector wields over the Indian economy can be seen from the fact that it is the second largest employer[123] in the country after agriculture and it contributes to 7 percent of the country's GDP.[124] The Indian real estate market is projected to touch $180 billion[125] by the year 2020. The construction industry ranks third among the 14 major sectors in terms of direct, indirect and induced effects in all sectors of the economy.

While the real estate sector can boast of all these milestones, yet another achievement that might not be so flaunt-worthy is the sector's status as possibly the largest receptacle of black money in India. An

---

[122] See 'India overtakes China, becomes biggest gold consumer: Survey', October 27, 2015, *The Economic Times,* PTI, http://economictimes.indiatimes.com/news/economy/indicators/india-overtakes-china-becomes-biggest-gold-consumer-survey/articleshow/49556979.cms

[123] See 'Demonetization: 'Housing prices already at lowest, no scope for correction,' says CREDAI', November 27, 2016, Daily News and Analysis (DNA), PTI, http://www.dnaindia.com/money/report-demonetization-housing-prices-already-at-lowest-no-scope-for-correction-says-credai-2277276

[124] Gross domestic product (GDP) is a monetary measure of the market value of all final goods and services produced in a period (quarterly or yearly).

[125] See 'Real Estate Industry in India', July, 2016, *India Brand Equity Foundation (IBEF),* http://www.ibef.org/industry/real-estate-india.aspx

The Cinderella Notes

Ambit Capital Research study[126] claims that black money funds around 30 percent of India's real estate sector. Unlike the case of gold or stock, though, there is no visible evidence or paper trail to establish the same. No wonder then that it is the most favoured option by hoarders who wish to invest their unaccounted for cash in an asset that can offer them stability, durability and value for money leaving hardly any trace of evidence. Just as the honest citizen wants to safeguard his hard earned, tax deducted income and savings by investing in real estate, the hoarder/black marketeer too wants to hoard his cash without worrying about storage or theft or, just as importantly, detection by the taxman. In the event of tax raids, while currency bundles and jewellery can be seized on the spot and taken into possession by the officials, real estate holdings are not so easily seized. Establishing the connection between unaccounted for income or black money and the acquisition/sale of property is no easy task and a considerable amount of legal wrangling will have to precede any move to attach real estate properties to an income tax dispute.

The Ambit study also indicated that the present government had been moving aggressively in conducting checks around gold transactions and it has become increasingly difficult to park unaccounted cash in the form of jewellery or bullion.

---

[126] See '30% of India's real estate sector funded by black money', June 06, 2016, *The Economic Times Realty*, PTI, http://realty.economictimes.indiatimes.com/news/industry/30-of-indias-real-estate-sector-funded-by-black-money/52614378

The Cinderella Notes

Towards the end of 2015, the Government of India made it mandatory for the PAN[127] number to be quoted for all transactions in excess of Rupees Two lakhs[128] from January 1, 2016. The earlier limit had been Rs 5 lakhs but the government believed that the lowering of the limit was warranted because of the rampant investing of black money in gold.

The All India Gems and Jewellery Trade Federation[129] expressed great dissatisfaction over the move. They believed that it would discriminate against those people who might not have PAN cards, for a variety of legitimate reasons. Jewellers in the country even went on strike in the first week of March, 2016 over the issue of the gold tax and also over the compulsory disclosure of PAN numbers. As expected, the sale of jewellery took a hit[130] in the first half of 2016 possibly because people preferred not to leave an official trail. Disclosing one's PAN number

---

[127] Permanent Account Number (PAN) is a ten-digit alphanumeric number, issued in the form of a laminated card, by the Income Tax Department in India, to any "person" who applies for it or to whom the department allots the number without an application.

[128] See 'PAN made mandatory for all transactions above Rs2 lakh', December 18, 2015, *Livemint*, Remya Nair,

http://www.livemint.com/Politics/UkFNyKXvjG8oE3QxzSM6bI/PAN-compulsory-for-opening-all-bank-accountsm-says-revenue.html

[129] See 'Jewellers unhappy over mandatory PAN on purchase of Rs 2 lakh' December 16, 2015, *The Economic Times*, PTI,

http://economictimes.indiatimes.com/wealth/personal-finance-news/jewellers-unhappy-over-mandatory-pan-on-purchase-of-rs-2-lakh/articleshow/50207202.cms

[130] See 'Jewellery industry hit by mandatory PAN Card for purchases over Rs 2 lakh', June 13, 2016, *Business Standard*, Gireesh Babu,

http://www.business-standard.com/article/companies/jewellery-industry-hit-by-mandatory-pan-card-for-purchases-over-rs-2-lakh-116061300696_1.html would mean an official record of the transaction. It was also possible that some people who'd previously invested in gold were now handicapped by the lack of a PAN Card. This could be because of legitimate reasons, like in the case of those with incomes that fall below the exemption limit or within the exempted category like, for example, agricultural income. The organized jewellery sector took a 50 percent hit in sales, a rather high percentage even after accounting for those without PAN Cards.

Likewise, stock market transactions also appeared to have been caught in the glare of scrutiny by the taxmen. A report[131] in the DNA newspaper revealed that the Income Tax (I-T) department was preparing to swoop down on stock market players following a probe revealing that alleged tax evaders were parking money in companies listed on the BSE[132] in order to avoid paying tax and shroud alleged black money. The IT department had collated information on the alleged dealings of individuals and companies through the securities transaction tax (STT) data submitted by NSE[133] and BSE for 2013-14 and 2014-15. According to reports of the I-T department, during 2014-15, trading of more than Rs 4,000 crore on BSE and nearly Rs 1,000 crore on NSE took place with the use of duplicate or bogus PAN card numbers. Such allegedly fraudulent dealings had only

---

[131] See 'IT dept to swoop down on tax evaders in stock market', October 13, 2016, *Daily News and Analysis (DNA)*, Dipu Rai, http://www.dnaindia.com/money/report-rs-30-lakh-crore-black-money-in-stock-markets-i-t-2263647
[132] Bombay Stock Exchange.
[133] National Stock Exchange of India.

benefited the stock market. The I-T department's figures for 2014-15 show that the stock market's turnover more than doubled, from Rs 32 lakh crore to Rs 66 lakh crore. In the same period, the number of alleged and potential tax evaders soared by about 150 percent. Documents in the DNA newspaper's possession revealed that investors had routed about Rs 30 lakh crore of funds through stock transactions in a year without disclosing their income sources.

All of this effectively meant that people, looking to invest unaccounted money, found physical assets a safer option than financial assets. For example, private equity money to the extent of $1.3 billion[134] flowed into the real estate sector in the half year ending June, 2015. There is a strong possibility that a significant percentage of this is black money stashed away in offshore accounts that has now been routed back into the country in the form of foreign private equity. Despite the real estate sector struggling over the last couple of years, there has been no dearth in the flow of private equity, with a 40 percent rise[135] at Rs 3,840 crores in the first quarter of 2016. This adds to the suspicion that a significant portion of illegal domestic money is held in the form of real estate.

[134] See 'Why Jaitley's threats won't work: All black money is in stock markets & real estate, too risky to touch', October 5, 2015, *First Post*, R Jagannathan, http://www.firstpost.com/business/why-jaitleys-threats-will-not-work-all-black-money-is-in-stock-markets-real-estate-too-risky-to-touch-2454746.html

[135] See 'Private equity investments in realty rise 40 per cent to Rs 3,840 crore in March quarter', May 07, 2016, *The Economic Times*, Ravi Teja Sharma, http://economictimes.indiatimes.com/wealth/real-estate/private-equity-investments-in-realty-rise-40-per-cent-to-rs-3840-crore-in-march-quarter/articleshow/52159685.cms

The primary criticism against demonetization was that the government was focused on flushing out the relatively small volume of the black money in circulation in the form of cash, while turning a blind eye to the reserves locked up in real estate or in offshore accounts. Going by a Finance Ministry report in 2012, real estate is said to account for almost 50 percent[136] of the black money market.

The real estate sector has a certain opacity factor that allows black money invested within to remain hidden, even while in plain sight. What this essentially means is that even while the black money is manifested in the form of the asset, making for a significant portion of its market value in fact, it remains invisible in terms of the property 'document' value.

The scope for undervaluing property in official documentation is what makes real estate the most sought after choice of the black money hoarders. The property guideline values in the land revenue registers of the revenue authorities are outdated and have not been aligned with market values in many years. So, people can easily get away with registering properties at a fraction of the market value, with only the guideline value, reflected in the property sale deed[137],

---

[136] See 'The Un-real Estate: The sector that is going to take the biggest hit', November 13, 2016, *The Indian Express*, Smita Nair, http://indianexpress.com/article/india/india-news-india/the-un-real-estate-demonetisation-process-100-500-rupee-note-narendra-modi-black-money-4372286/

[137] This is typically the guideline value set by the state government.

being settled through a banking transaction—the remaining is usually paid in the form of black money.

While real estate deals are indeed a preferred means to camouflage unaccounted cash reserves by converting them to a fixed asset, the physical cash merely changes hands. The velocity of money then comes into play as it passes numerous hands in its travel through the economy, multiplying manifold the levels of tax evasion. More often than not, the cash component of a real estate deal is higher than the property 'document' value that is settled through a banking transaction.

In the wake of demonetization, it is believed that the real estate sector will take a huge hit given that all accumulated cash reserves of black money, in the form of high value currencies, have been rendered non-fungible. Propequity, an online subscription based real estate data and analytics platform, predicts a fall of up to 30 percent[138] in housing prices and a loss to the sector to the tune of Rs 8 lakh crore within the next year. However, opinion is divided on that with some others feeling that no drastic fall is possible given that property prices in key markets have remained stagnant due to a three-year slowdown in the real estate sector.[139]

---

[138] See 'Demonetisation: Housing prices to drop up to 30%, wiping Rs 8 lakh cr in value', November 24, 2016, *First Post*, PTI, http://www.firstpost.com/business/demonetisation-housing-prices-to-drop-up-to-30-wiping-rs-8-lakh-cr-in-value-3122946.html
[139] See 'Opinion divided over impact of demonetisation on real estate prices', November 21, 2016, *Livemint*, Bidya Sapam, http://www.livemint.com/Companies/o2fVwCBoD8rrJv12XaENm

The Benami Transactions Amendment Act 2016[140] could also serve as a further deterrent to investing black money in real estate. A *benami*[141] transaction is defined as a transaction wherein a property is held by or transferred in the name of a person but has been provided or paid for by another person. The definition also includes property transactions where i) a transaction has been made under a fictitious name; ii) the owner is not aware or denies knowledge of the ownership of the property; iii) the person providing the property is not traceable.

Benami transactions originally came into being post the Central Government's enactment of the Urban Land (Ceiling and Regulation) Act in1976 and the Agricultural Land Ceiling Acts enacted by the various state governments with a view to ensuring equitable distribution of land amongst the people. In order to protect their existing land holdings, people transferred sections of their property to the names of their relatives and trusted confidantes to be held in trust until such time as they needed to liquidate it. Likewise, those making fresh acquisitions, particularly using black money, also preferred to invest in the

---

L/Opinion-divided-over-impact-of-demonetisation-on-real-estate.html

[140] See 'The Benami Transactions (Prohibition) Amendment Act, 2016, No. 43 Of 2016, August 10, 2016, *Ministry Of Law And Justice*, The Gazette of India',
http://www.prsindia.org/uploads/media/Benami/Benami%20Trans actions%20Act,%202016.pdf

[141] Benami is a Persian language word that means "without name" or "no name". In this Act, the word is used to define a transaction in which the real beneficiary is not the one in whose name the property is purchased. As a result, the person in whose name the property is purchased is just a mask for the real beneficiary.

names of family members and friends with a view to escape the scrutiny of the tax authorities as well as the revenue officials. The Urban Land Ceiling Act was repealed in 1999 while the Agricultural Land Reform legislations remain in operation in several Indian states.

The Benami Transactions Amendment Act 2016, basically an amendment to the Benami Transactions (Prohibition) Act of 1988, proposed the creation of an authority for the acquisition of property acquired through *benami*[142] means, and also laid down punitive measures including possible imprisonment or penalties or both. However, in keeping with the thought of influencing and enabling compliance rather than enforcing it, the Income Declaration Scheme (IDS), 2016 was implemented for the voluntary declaration of undisclosed income, including disclosure of non-cash assets like moveable or immoveable assets, gold and jewellery. The undisclosed income was to be taxed at a flat rate of 45 percent.[143] As per Circular No. 17 of 2016 dated 20th May, 2016 and Circular No. 24 of 2016 dated 27th June, 2016, such assets were accorded immunity[144] under the Income-tax Act, 1961, the

---

[142] Benami is a Persian language word that means "without name" or "no name". In this Act, the word is used to define a transaction in which the real beneficiary is not the one in whose name the property is purchased. As a result, the person in whose name the property is purchased is just a mask for the real beneficiary.

[143] See 'The Income Declaration Scheme 2016 to open from 1st June 2016', May 14, 2016, *Press Information Bureau*, Government of India, Ministry of Finance,
http://pib.nic.in/newsite/PrintRelease.aspx?relid=145360

[144] See 'Clarifications on the Income Declaration Scheme, 2016', June 30, 2016, Circular No. 25 of 2016, Government of India, Ministry of

Wealth-tax Act, 1957 and the Benami Transactions (Prohibition) Act, 1988 providing certain conditions were met.

The same provisions apply to the disclosure of gold and jewellery also. By laying down that with non-disclosure, an assessee runs the risk of forfeiture, the punitive aspect has also been addressed. Backed up by income tax scrutiny and investigations, these serve as sufficient motivation to declare all undisclosed income in whatever form, and serve as a fair deterrent for the future. The Income Tax department notified[145] that the Benami Transactions (Prohibition) Amendment Act, 2016 (BTP Amendment Act), will come into force from November 1, 2016.

In addition, from the beginning of 2016, the Government has been insisting on PAN[146] numbers

---

Finance, Department of Revenue Central Board of Direct Taxes, http://www.incometaxindia.gov.in/communications/circular/circular252016.pdf

[145] See 'Benami Transactions (Prohibition) Amendment Act, 2016 To Come In To Effect From Tomorrow [Read Bill]', October 31, 2016, *LiveLaw.in*, Vidushi Sahani, http://www.livelaw.in/benami-transactions-prohibition-amendment-act-2016-come-effect-tomorrow-read-bill/

[146] See 'PAN/TAN', http://www.incometaxindia.gov.in/Pages/pan.aspx Permanent Account Number (PAN) is a ten-digit alphanumeric number, issued in the form of a laminated card, by the Income Tax Department, to any "person" who applies for it or to whom the department allots the number without an application. PAN enables the department to link all transactions of the "person" with the department. These transactions include tax payments, TDS/TCS credits, returns of income/wealth/gift/FBT, specified transactions, correspondence,

for gold and jewellery transactions upwards of Rs 2 lakh, term deposits upwards of Rs 5 lakh, shares and stocks valued at upward of Rs 1 lakh and real estate valued at over Rs 10 lakh. This is to facilitate the easy retrieval of information and to facilitate matching of information relating to investment, raising of loans and other business activities of taxpayers collected through various sources, both internal as well as external. This step is expected to help in detecting and combating tax evasion and also, widening of the tax base.

Given the critical role of the real estate sector in contributing to GDP growth, and also its role as the second largest employment generator, the sector's well-being is crucial to the health of the larger economy.

The Chairman of the Confederation of Real Estate Developers Associations of India, Pradeep Jain, called for reforms[147] to the sector, considering how critical the sector was for the Government to achieve growth targets of 7-8 percent per annum. The sector is said to impact more than 250 manufacturing and services industries including steel and cement. Apart from industry level concessions, tax rebates and project finance, certain other concessions need to be

---

and so on. PAN, thus, acts as an identifier for the "person" with the tax department.

[147] See 'Reforms in real estate key to GDP growth: Credai', January 6, 2013, *The Hindu Business Line*,
http://www.thehindubusinessline.com/news/real-estate/reforms-in-real-estate-key-to-gdp-growth-credai/article4279859.ece

extended to ensure the health of the sector in the interest of the investors as well as the economy.

The above apart, what is critical is an immediate rationalization of guideline values[148] of properties in the revenue department records, making them more in tune with the actual rates that prevail in the markets. Even where parties to a transaction are willing to record the entire sale value[149], they are often dissuaded by the revenue officials themselves on the grounds that it would set a precedent and prove a deterrent to other parties wanting to avail themselves of the benefits of low property guideline values. A rationalization of the property guideline values with the prevailing market rates would force the transacting parties to register the sale at actual cost rather than a fraction of it, thereby eliminating the black money component in the transaction. That is the key point that needs to be noted here. And with rationalization, it would become next to impossible for the sector to absorb black money the way it is doing currently.

A rule of thumb can be applied for correcting the property guideline value—increase the guideline value by 4 to 5 times for rural areas, 3 to 3.5 times for peri-urban areas and 2 to 2.5 times for urban areas. As someone with grassroots level experience across the country, this is a simple heuristic I suggest

---

[148] This needs to be undertaken by the respective state governments.
[149] In many cases, the seller is ready to accept all money via the bank but the buyers are reluctant because they cannot show a proper source for the monies provided. This then forces legitimate tax abiding sellers also to accept black (unaccounted) money.

to arrive at initial estimates for revising the guideline value. These can subsequently be adjusted as per actual demand.

Stamp duties and registration charges are the other important components in any real estate transaction and they too need to be rationalized[150] across India to further eliminate the black money component. Both these revenue receipts accrue to the individual states and the Central government has no jurisdiction over them. Going by 2014–15 budget estimates, the total revenue accruing to the states from stamp duty and registration charges stood at Rs 98,040 crores[151], at a little under 8 percent of the total state revenues from all sources. They rank third among all direct state revenues, after state sales tax (43 percent) and state excise duties (8 percent).

Since stamp duty and registration fees are calculated as a percentage of the total value of the transaction, rationalizing guideline values will result in a huge increase in the transaction costs related to any property purchase. Since it is incumbent on the buyer to pay stamp duty and registration fees, he would prefer to undervalue the consideration quoted in the deed of sale to save on the costs of stamp duty and

---

[150] See 'Slash stamp duty to clean up real estate sector: Assocham', November 14, 2016, *The Economic Times*, PTI, http://economictimes.indiatimes.com/wealth/real-estate/slash-stamp-duty-to-clean-up-real-estate-sector-assocham/articleshow/55413511.cms?from=mdr

[151] See 'Indian Public Finance Statistics 2014-2015', July, 2015 *Ministry Of Finance, Department Of Economic Affairs and Economic Division*, Government of India, http://finmin.nic.in/reports/IPFStat201415.pdf

registration charges. The current stamp duty rates range[152] from as low as 4 percent to as high as 10 percent.

The National Housing Bank, which is a subsidiary of the RBI, must work along with IG of Registrars in different states to rationalize and reduce stamp duties. At no point or in no state should stamp duty be in excess of 2 percent of the guideline value in line with the best practices the world over. Registration fees must also be scrapped in totality.

In the current situation of unrealistic guideline values and exorbitant stamp duty charges, people will resort to undervaluing the properties to avoid paying taxes and this will only result in a loss to the exchequer. This will also have a cascading effect[153] since the transaction value will have a direct bearing on other taxes like property tax, wealth tax and gift tax.

A recursive cycle will be set off where, in order to avoid revealing the existence of this black money, the individual or the company must utilize it in ways that maintain secrecy. The monies derived from undervaluation/evasion cannot be brought into the books of accounts and hence cannot be used for legitimate or official transactions. Such monies

---

[152] See appendix 10 for a listing of stamp duty rates across states.

[153] See 'Stamp Duties in Indian States: A Case for Reform', September 2004, *World Bank Policy Research Working Paper 3413*, James Alm, Patricia Annez, and Arbind Modi, http://documents.worldbank.org/curated/en/775111468750283848/pdf/WPS3413.pdf

accumulated through such unaccounted means produce a cascading effect through the entire production process, as activities must continue to remain hidden. Put differently, the underreporting incentive in property sale and stamp duties feeds the "black economy" by driving more such unaccounted money and resources into the sector, which then multiplies even further as it is used to fuel a variety of transactions in the black or the parallel economy.

For example, the most frequent recipients of the unaccounted funds would be property builders who, in turn, will continue to have incentives to circulate this unaccounted cash in the parallel (black) economy. And the further this money circulates, it fuels a whole range of other transactions that fall out of the ambit of the tax system. For example, cash payments to raw materials suppliers result in loss of sales tax and excise duties. Likewise, property builders who receive the payments as cash avoid showing these receipts as income and hence, evade income tax. Taken together, all these recipients of the unaccounted black (cash) money start the cycle of buying goods and services in the black economy, all of which continue to escape the tax net with a huge cascading effect. The net result is that not only are stamp duty and registration fees avoided but a whole range of taxes are lost both by the central and state governments. Also, black attracts more black in the sense that the scope for undervalued transactions and tax evasion thereon attract more and more people who are looking for ways to 'unofficially' invest their unaccounted for wealth.

Effectively, if rationalization of guideline values and stamp duty charges happens, it directly eliminates the scope for a black money component in real estate transactions, since there is no scope to conceal or evade.

The Real Estate (Regulation and Development) Bill,[154] 2016, which became an act on May 1, has kick-started the process of putting in place an institutional infrastructure to protect the interests of home buyers in India. From an honest, tax-paying buyer's perspective, this is a welcome step. If the revision of guideline values is also effected across various states of India, it would effectively mean that he would be able to reflect the entire value of his acquisition in his book of assets and also raise loans from the formal financial institutions to finance his transaction. Corruption at the level of the planning bodies[155] also needs addressing, since builders/developers end up passing on the bribes paid to hasten the process of acquiring permits/licenses/permissions to the buyers in the form of the black money component of the sale price.

Yet another aspect that needs consideration is the percentage of sale proceeds that a seller would need to pay into the exchequer in the form of capital gains

---

[154] See 'Real Estate Bill is an act now, may protect home buyers', May 02, 2016, *The Economic Times,* Ravi Teja Sharma, http://economictimes.indiatimes.com/wealth/real-estate/real-estate-bill-is-an-act-now-may-protect-home-buyers/articleshow/52069308.cms

[155] This would include state, regional and local planning bodies that provide permissions for plot development and building construction.

tax if it is a non-agricultural asset, or as a higher income tax in certain other scenarios like short term capital gains. There are exemptions to long term capital gains if the sale proceeds are reinvested within a stipulated time frame. Overall, a rationalization of capital gains tax too would help in keeping the real estate sector black money free.

Tax reforms on all these fronts might also yield unexpected benefits in the form of retaining some portion of domestic capital that is otherwise invested in real estate outside India. India[156] ranks eighth from the top in a list of countries by the amount of land acquired abroad. Indian companies have been among the biggest investors in land in countries like Cambodia, Indonesia, Madagascar, Kenya and Ethiopia. The Indian government is itself a major investor in land abroad, especially in East Africa, and has acquired over 4.8 million hectares worldwide spread across nine deals. Indians are also the largest non-Arab investors in Dubai. However, it is the West that holds the most attraction for Indian companies investing in property abroad. The Lodha Group plans to invest over £5 billion in the coming years in developing property in London, which will be the largest FDI in real estate that the UK will have ever received. In FY 2013-14, the Indians were ranked fourth, only behind the Canadians, Chinese and Mexicans, in investing in properties in US cities.

---

[156] See 'Indian direct investment', June 29, 2015, *The Indian Express,* Christophe Jaffrelot,
http://indianexpress.com/article/opinion/columns/indian-direct-investment/

While on the one hand, India continues to try to attract FDI[157] in real estate, here we have a reverse flow happening. Though there may be a certain element of prestige associated with the acquisition of real estate in prime global spots, the 'messy' state of affairs in Indian real estate is surely a reason too. The lack of transparency in deals, the high levels of unaccounted money and the degree of corruption encountered in the process of acquiring approvals and permits for real estate projects, from the revenue and the planning authorities, all of these possibly serve as deterrents in attracting FDI as also helping to retain domestic capital within the country.

In the wake of demonetization, it is going to be extremely difficult to structure real estate deals with a black money component. The reserves are lost for now and it might take time to build them up all over again, except for what might have already been routed out of the country to be brought back through other means.

Overall, the importance of the real estate sector in kick-starting the Indian economy—which is bound to suffer a slowdown post demonetization—cannot be stressed upon enough. There are allied industries like construction, cement, steel and others that feed into the real estate sector. Increased activity in all of

---

[157] See 'Indian Government Announces FDI in Real Estate to Benefit the Real Estate Growth', November 17, 2015, *Business Wire*, The Hindu Business Line,
http://www.thehindubusinessline.com/news/real-estate/indian-government-announces-fdi-in-real-estate-to-benefit-the-real-estate-growth/article7886880.ece

these industries would contribute to the sector's growth and thereby enhance its contribution to overall employment and income generation.

If the suggested reforms in this chapter are carried out in the interim and corruption eliminated from the process of acquiring licenses and approval of real estate project permits, and if compliance with safety standards and other requisites are ensured, the realty sector might be able to survive the drying up of the lubricant that kept it well-oiled and find ways to reinvent itself without losing its inherent strengths.

CHAPTER 5

To Pay Or Not To Pay

If the mythical bogeyman struck terror in our hearts while we were children, the all too real taxman strikes fear in our hearts even after we are all grown up. Not even the most honest and upright amongst us can claim to have a particular affinity for the species. The farther away they are, the greater at peace we are. And yet, their tentacles reach out and ensnare us all the time, in ways that we sometimes don't even notice. Then there are the times when we feel that we are directly under their microscopic scrutiny, like cornered organisms that lie trapped under their gaze. Either which way, there is no hope of escape.

Why such an aversion to the taxman, though, and why the desperation to get away from their scrutiny? Why do the palms of even the mightiest amongst us sweat in their presence? It is obviously because the taxman's job is to take away from us a portion of our hard earned money. Their justifications of common good simply don't convince us but we are not empowered to resist.

Wikipedia defines **tax**[158] (from the <u>Latin</u> <u>taxo</u>) as a financial charge or other levy imposed upon a taxpayer (an individual or <u>legal entity</u>) by a <u>state</u> or the functional equivalent of a state to fund various public expenditures. Taxation is not some novel phenomenon that came in with the advent of modern society; rather the principle dates back to ancient times.

The great Indian epic *Mahabharata* offers advice on taxation to the ruler of the day:

> "The king should take wealth from his subjects at the proper time... Like an intelligent man milking his cow every day, the king should milk his kingdom every day. As the bee collects honey from flowers gradually, without causing harm to the tree; the king should draw wealth gradually from his kingdom for storing it." — **Bhishma's counsel to Yudhishthira.** (Mahabharata, Book 12: Santi Parva: Rajadharmanusasana Parva)

A Sumerian tablet dating back to 2500 BC makes a reference[159] to payment of tax, which was rather rightly referred to as 'burden'. In ancient Mesopotamia, since coined money wasn't prevalent, ancient households paid taxes in kind, and all through the year. Merchants were required to pay tolls, duty fees and other taxes while transporting goods from one region to another. Not surprisingly, along with references to levies, there is mention of

---

[158] See *Charles E. McLure, Jr.* "Taxation" , Britannica, Retrieved 3 March 2015— - https://en.wikipedia.org/wiki/Tax

[159] See 'Taxes in the Ancient World', *University of Pennsylvania Almanac*, December 2nd 2016, *University of Pennsylvania Almanac*, http://www.upenn.edu/almanac/v48/n28/AncientTaxes.html

tax evasion too. The Mesopotamian merchants frequently took to smuggling to escape the tax dragnet. A letter dated around 1900 B.C. details the consequences of such evasion, as written by a trader from the head office to his employee:

> "Irra's son sent smuggled goods to Pushuken but his smuggled goods were intercepted. The Palace then threw Pushuken in jail! The guards are strong...please don't smuggle anything else!"

Clearly, people didn't enjoy paying taxes back then, just as they don't today. When more and more people find ways to evade the taxman by not bringing their income/wealth or a portion of it into the books, such unaccounted monies slowly accumulate and fuel a whole new parallel (shadow) economy that subsists alongside the formal economy. No portion of the income derived from it is contributed to state expenditure on 'common good'.

Like their counterparts in history, most governments choose tax raids and punitive justice as the weapons to be unleashed on such hoarders of cash. The Government of India has chosen the not so commonly used weapon of demonetization, for the third time in the last seventy years. The stated objective, of course, is to slay the demon of black money, along with lesser demons like counterfeit currency and bring to light the 'underground economy' that had remained under the spell of the 'black money' demon.

Suddenly, a whole stash of black money held in the form of the SBNs has ceased to be legal tender. The only hope of redemption is if it surrenders itself to the formal financial system, which would replace it with valid currency. Not all of it, though. The holders of the 'black money' will have to lose a significant portion of it to the much reviled taxman, much more than they would have had to if they had thought to disclose it right when it had accrued.

On the night of demonetization, Prime Minister Modi announced that a 200 percent penalty would be levied on such disclosed monies, the source of which was not explained to the satisfaction of the tax authorities. Along with the existing tax rate of 30 percent, and the additional penalty of 200 percent of the tax to be paid, the final effective rate of tax would be 90 percent. In effect, the hoarders would be left with a mere 10 percent in value of the black money they had accumulated and would find the taxman breathing down their necks possibly for perpetuity.

Just as they adopted creative ways to hide their accumulated 'black money' from the public gaze, in the form of gold, stocks and, more often, real estate, the evaders scurried around in the days following demonetization, trying their best to save as much as they could of their stashed away black money reserves. There were hurried purchases of gold with backdated bills and purchases of foreign exchange at a premium. Salaries and other dues were paid in advance and memberships of exclusive spas and gymnasiums were renewed. There were also reports that crores of rupees worth of currency was either burnt or dumped into rivers and/or garbage bins.[160]

Since it was declared that deposits under Rs 2.5 lakhs the prevailing income tax exemption limit, would not attract the taxman's scrutiny, there were those who hurriedly hired money mules or used their own employees[161] to deposit the cash into their accounts in return for a commission or to get the notes exchanged across the counters at banks/post offices. The Jan Dhan accounts,[162] opened as part of the Government's drive to bring those excluded from the formal financial system within its fold, were targeted by businessmen seeking ways in which to surreptitiously convert their black money reserves. There were even reports of bank staff colluding on such transactions. Touts[163] were seen offering to

---

[160] See 'One week after demonetisation announcement, crores of old currency notes burned, destroyed, dumped', November 16, 2016, *Business Standard*, BS Web Team, http://www.business-standard.com/article/current-affairs/demonetisation-effect-one-week-after-announcement-crores-old-currency-notes-burned-destroyed-dumped-116111600335_1.html

[161] See 'Misuse of bank account for black money deposit to invite govt action', November 18, 2016, *Hindustan Times*, Mahua Venkatesh, http://www.hindustantimes.com/india-news/misuse-of-bank-account-for-black-money-deposit-to-invite-govt-action/story-NmqcCcCsz5pmJGy2E1oHGJ.html

[162] See 'Dead since birth, Jan Dhan accounts now flush with cash', November 12, 2016, *The Economic Times*, Yogesh Dubey and Aditya Dev, http://economictimes.indiatimes.com/industry/banking/finance/banking/dead-since-birth-jan-dhan-accounts-now-flush-with-cash/articleshow/55385716.cms

[163] See 'A Delhi Trader Reveals How Touts Are Helping People Convert Their Black Cash Into New Notes', November 25, 2016, *Scoop Whoop*, Swati Goel Sharma, https://www.scoopwhoop.com/A-

exchange the currency for a fee, sometimes as high as 40 percent of the value. Clearly, people were willing to lose a significant portion of the money to touts or others rather than face the wrath of the taxman. Of course, there was also the issue of expediency, since deposit/exchange of the SBNs with banks involved standing for long hours in queues and would not serve their need for immediate cash.

The government soon realized the tactics that people were resorting to in a bid to avoid coming under tax scrutiny and being penalized. Limits were imposed on over the counter currency exchange and warnings were issued that *benami*[164] account deposits would come under scrutiny and face penalty.[165]

So why do people go to such extremes and risk legal action in a bid to avoid paying tax and why is the government going to such extreme measures to ensure they cough up what is due, and even more as fines?

In the context of a developing economy like India, where large sections of the population are still in

---

Delhi-Trader-Reveals-How-Touts-Are-Converting-Peoples-Black-Money-Into-New-Notes/#.ub4wslv3b

[164] Benami is a Persian language word that means "without name" or "no name". The word is used to define a transaction in which the real beneficiary is not the one in whose name the transaction has been conducted. As a result, the person in whose name the transaction is conducted is just a mask for the real beneficiary.

[165] See 'Demonetisation: Misuse of bank account for black money deposit to invite govt action', November 24, 2016, *The Indian Express*, PTI, http://indianexpress.com/article/india/india-news-india/demonetisation-government-to-prosecute-jan-dhan-account-holders-for-black-money-deposit-4382373/

need of state intervention to gain access to basic amenities and services, public expenditure on infrastructure building is necessarily huge. This is also because of the high degree of inequity that prevails, wherein 45 percent of India's wealth is controlled by her millionaires with the figure shooting up to 54 percent if the NRI[166] millionaires are included.[167]

With such a lopsided distribution of wealth, the State's role in restoring some degree of equity assumes significance and rightfully so. To enable the majority of its citizens to gain access to resources and services that they might not be able to afford, the State has to necessarily create public infrastructure in areas like food supplies, drinking water, health, education, transport and sanitation among others, which are integral to the basic quality of life. Besides, there are other state controlled areas like power generation,[168] roads and highway building,

---

[166] A Non-Resident Indian (NRI) is a citizen of India who holds an Indian passport and has temporarily emigrated to another country for six months or more for employment, residence, education or any other purpose.

[167] This is revealed in a report of New World Wealth, a wealth research firm. See 'Yes, India has massive income inequality—but it isn't the second-most unequal country in the world', September 06, 2016, *Scroll.in*, Mayank Jain, http://scroll.in/article/815751/yes-india-has-massive-income-inequality-but-it-isnt-the-second-most-unequal-country-in-the-world

[168] Although, in the last several years, power generation and transmission has been privatized to some extent, the state can still be said to be a large player in the power sector. With regard to infrastructure in general, Public Private Partnerships (PPP's) are getting to be the norm these days. However, none of these diminish the important role that the state has to play in facilitating greater quality of access to these services for the poor, marginalized and excluded populations.

communication networks etc., that are crucial to the country's economic growth. Given that the state plays a hugely important role in the provision of some of these infrastructural services, the government undoubtedly needs to levy charges on its citizens commensurate with the usage of these services. Yet, the levies need to be heavily subsidized given that the services would be otherwise removed from the reach of the poor.

And if these subsidies are to be made possible, then the state needs to target the wealth of the rich to finance the same. That is precisely the reason why income tax slabs are created to allow for higher taxation of the economically privileged. It is on the same basis that the services availed by the well-to-do are often differentially priced, be it charges for electricity and water or additional taxes in case of property and/or wealth taxes.

Now, when large amounts of money float in the parallel or the black economy, whether in the form of cash or as assets, they are effectively monies that are being kept away from financing investment of infrastructure and services, including those for the poor. Given that a major portion of the black money is again concentrated in the hands of the wealthy, it follows that the existing inequities in the country are being perpetuated, since these monies are most often converted to assets or splurged on conspicuous and wasteful consumption expenditure.[169] In the interests of not allowing one section of society to grow at the

---

[169] There are many examples that can be provided here.

expense of all others, the principle of taxation that lawfully pinches the pockets of the rich to line the stomachs of the poor would seem fair and just.

Flipping sides, the same principle might not appear so fair to those who don't see the need to ensure equitable distribution. For them, their income is a product of their own efforts, possibly aided by ancestral wealth, and so they do not feel the need to share the same with someone who is not blessed with similar privilege, be it in terms of circumstances of birth or social status or skill. Wealth breeds a sense of entitlement and so, many times, the wealthy do not even understand the rationale of subsidies. They see it as a case of their rights being compromised when differential pricing is adopted on the supply of essential services like power and water for example. Most often they do not make use of public infrastructure in areas like education, health and transportation and fail to see the rationale behind why *they* are required to contribute to the establishment or the operation of such infrastructure by levying higher taxes on their income. To put it simply, they do not see value for their money.

So they find ways to escape or short circuit the tax system, be it by under-quoting their income, undervaluing the properties they buy or sell, through buying products and services without proper bills and receipts and so on.

There can be no better illustration of this 'escapist attitude' with regard to taxation than the immediate kneejerk responses that the demonetization announcement elicited, which have been detailed earlier in the book.

On November 29, 2016, the Taxation Laws (Second Amendment) Bill,[170] 2016, was passed in the lower house of the Indian parliament, bringing radical changes to the taxation/penalty on undisclosed income. When the demonetization announcement came, the tax[171] proposed on the unaccounted demonetized cash was close to 90 percent (tax plus penalty of 200 percent). With the amendment, it was revised to a tax of 30 percent of the income declared, a 33 percent additional surcharge on the tax amount, and a further penalty of 10 per cent of the declared income. In all, the tax liability including penalties totalled up to about 50 percent. Besides the tax component, the amendment also clarified that 25 percent of the declared income was to be deposited in an interest-free deposit scheme to be notified by the government in consultation with the RBI. All of this was applicable provided the person concerned voluntarily disclosed it.

If, however, such unaccounted income were to be discovered subsequent to December 30, 2016, a flat

---

[170] See 'Amid disruptions & uproar, Bill to tax deposits passed in Lok Sabha', November 29, 2016, *The Hindu,* Special Correspondent, http://www.thehindu.com/news/national/Amid-disruptions-uproar-Bill-to-tax-deposits-passed-in-Lok-Sabha/article16720245.ece

[171] See 'Demonetisation: Deposits above Rs 2.5 lakh to face tax, penalty on mismatch, says Hasmukh Adhia', November 10, 2016, *ENS Economic Bureau,* The Indian Express, http://indianexpress.com/article/india/india-news-india/demonetisation-rs-500-rs-1000-deposits-above-rs-2-5-lakh-tax-penalty-on-mismatch-hasmukh-adhia-4367184/

tax of 60 percent, a further surcharge of 25 percent on the tax amount, and a possible 10 percent penalty at the discretion of the assessing officer would apply. The total levy on undeclared income or assets could then be as high as 85 percent.

Clearly, the intent of the government was (a good one) to try to retrieve from the economy as much as possible of the black money in circulation as cash. After all, having it thrown into fire or water did not really serve anyone's purpose.

The amendment seemed to receive a thumbs up[172] from the experts who believed that this could be an incentive for more of the defaulters to declare their unaccounted income.

It is going to take until the end of December,[173] which is when this last chance at voluntary disclosure will also close, to arrive at a final figure on the total value of SBNs surrendered to the system. Figures released by the RBI indicate that, between November 10 and December 10, banks saw SBNs worth Rs

---

[172] See 'Income Tax Act amendment a 'win-win', to boost govt revenues: Experts', November 28, 2016, *The Indian Express*, PTI, http://indianexpress.com/article/india/india-news-india/income-tax-act-amendment-a-win-win-to-boost-govt-revenues-experts/
[173] As per the original demonetization notification, SBNs can be deposited after the expiry of the December 30 deadline at specified RBI offices until a later date to be notified by them. But the scheme for voluntary disclosure of the income ends on December 30, 2016. See 'Withdrawal of Legal Tender Status for Rs 500 and Rs1000 Notes: RBI Notice'. November 8, 2016, RBI Press Release, https://rbi.org.in/Scripts/BS_PressReleaseDisplay.aspx?prid=38520

12.44 lakh crore[174] being deposited and/or exchanged. What percentage of the deposits is black money is something that would need to be ascertained.

While the demonetization exercise might help to mop up the cash component of 'black money' in circulation in the market for the time being, it is not a long-term solution to the problem. A more permanent solution would be a rationalization of the taxation system and also an attitudinal change[175] in the people apropos taxation.

So, how do we influence attitudinal change and, how do we reconcile a sense of justice with a sense of entitlement? For, unless this rationalization happens, black money or the parallel economy is going nowhere.

Attitudinal change requires a two-pronged approach. To begin with, you need to make the taxation system more rational and less punitive and secondly, you must make the taxpayer feel that paying taxes is worth his while. The present cash crunch seems to have created a certain loss of confidence, leading people to keep a tight hold on cash in their hand, to wait, watch and play it safe with regard to spending it. The RBI[176] has appealed to the people not to

---

[174] See 'Shri R. Gandhi and Shri S. S. Mundra, RBI Deputy Governors brief Agencies on Currency Issues: Edited Transcript', December 13, 2016, *Reserve Bank of India*, Press Release, https://rbi.org.in/Scripts/BS_PressReleaseDisplay.aspx?prid=38886
[175] That attitudes influence behaviors goes without saying.
[176] See 'Enough cash available, don't hoard, RBI tells people', November 13, 2016, *Hindustan Times*, Beena Parmar,

hoard cash and has cautioned them that this would only make the situation worse. The government has also repeatedly tried to reassure[177] them of the adequacy of cash reserves. A dip in purchasing power, even if self-imposed, has the potential to lead to an overall (at least, temporary) slowdown with the wheels of the economy juddering to a screeching halt.

India can ill-afford a slow down at this time, right when things appeared to be looking up on the economic front and when the economies of competitors like China are displaying sluggish tendencies. The government needs to put the confidence back in the economy, make people loosen their purse strings and go back to their spending ways. For this to happen, the government needs to give them some bit of good news, a hope for the future and put them in the mood to celebrate.

What better good news can a taxpayer hope for than a tax cut? To be told that he will have more discretionary income at his disposal. The immediate way forward then is a reform of the income tax structure. While it might not apply to the current financial year, the good news on tax cuts for the following financial year must reach their ears in double quick time. A future saving will certainly

---

http://www.hindustantimes.com/business-news/enough-cash-available-don-t-hoard-rbi-tells-people/story-QIJZzNN4dxYjUvBD3irZcL.html

[177] See 'Demonetisation: RBI has more than adequate cash, says Arun Jaitley', December 20, 2016, Catch News, Speed News Desk, http://www.catchnews.com/national-news/demonetisation-rbi-has-more-than-adequate-cash-says-arun-jaitley-1482222521.html

provide the right impetus and confidence for the people to give up the austere ways that demonetization has pushed them to. Income tax proposals have that kind of power over an economy, the power to make or break it.

In the long term, taxation laws need to be simplified. The taxman needs a makeover, from being the real world's bogeyman to someone who will counsel and handhold you through the process of filing your tax returns, rather than frighten you with the power of his position. Wherever and whenever possible, positive reinforcement rather than the threat of punitive action must be used to influence attitudes and bring about behavioural changes. A transparent and simple tax system can go a long way to helping people negotiate their way through it, rather than be lost in the quagmire that it is presently.

Taxation should be *pareto optimal*—it should neither diminish the drive for enterprise nor should it result in huge inequities due to the hoarding of money by a select few. An unduly high tax rate and low exemption limits are constraining factors on consumption and enterprise. That is why having a transparent and forward looking tax system is critical for any economy.

Once the The Goods and Services Tax (GST)[178] is rolled out in 2017, most of the existing taxes will

---

[178] See 'Goods and Services Tax (GST) Bill, explained', October 19, 2016, Indian Express, Express News Service,
http://indianexpress.com/article/explained/gst-bill-parliament-what-is-goods-services-tax-economy-explained-2950335/

merge into a single system of taxation, thereby rationalizing and simplifying the implementation of indirect taxes to a large degree. Hence, we will restrict the discussion in this chapter to direct taxes and more specifically, to income tax.

What are the criteria that enable a system to be a forward looking transparent tax system?

First: **simplicity.**
Second: **transaction cost.**
Third: **ease of implementation.**
Fourth: **openness.**
Fifth: **equitability.**

Students of accounting and commerce often complain about the difficulty in clearing their Income Tax exams, such is the level of complexity in interpretation and application of the rules that frame the system. There is often disagreement even amongst audit professionals over exemptions, limits and deductions. No wonder then that the common man feels highly pressurized through the process of filing his tax returns. Starting February through July, the salaried classes have a haunted look about them as they grapple with the demons of tax returns. If they already feel the pinch of having to pay a tax, which they feel is not entirely fair, the complexity of the process only adds further aggravation.

The complexity of the task directly feeds into transaction cost as the amount of time, effort and resources that the tax filing process demands is inversely proportional to the benefits that the tax-payers feel they derive from the process.

The complex nature of the taxation process demands considerable time and resources from the system itself in order for the tax laws to be effectively implemented. If the structural issues are an impediment to the ease of implementation, the rather dated tools available to the taxman are another big problem. Although the methods used to identify potential defaulters have been updated in terms of technology, their inclusion in data gathering continues to remain a work-in-progress.

The element of secrecy associated with the process is yet another issue, although it is possibly linked to the threat of punitive force that is used to ensure compliance and of course, to the felt need to evade the process to whatever degree possible. There is a shroud of secrecy confining the process and the implementation, and the taxman is this mysterious figure that one is always fearing and constantly trying to second guess.

While India has achieved much in its income tax proposals from the 1970s, there is still a lot more left to be done. Most budgets tend to address the issue superficially, more in terms of exemption limits and tax rates. Not much thought is given to simplifying the procedures and processes involved in making it less of a cumbersome, unpleasant chore.

The Cinderella Notes

In the context of realising the objectives of demonetization, tax reforms need to address both the complex process of filing tax returns and also the tax rates applicable to different income slabs.

At this juncture, it would be pertinent to take a cue from the forward looking tax system of a country like New Zealand.[179] Its tax systems are ranked amongst the most progressive and easy to navigate in the world. New Zealand went through a major program of tax reform in the 1980s. The top marginal rate of income tax[180] stands at 33 percent for incomes above NZ$70,000 and companies and corporates are charged at a flat 28 percent. To implement something similar, some number crunching is required to try to calculate an effective tax rate.

A pre-requisite for tax reform suggestions is a thorough and complete understanding of the existing systems and processes. Furthermore, the magnitude of impact that is likely to occur needs to be understood, given the quantum of resources generated as taxes.

A look at the estimates of income tax revenue of the government should give us a fair idea of the kind of monies accrued. The revenue from taxes on

---

[179] See 'Taxes', *Newzealand Now*,
https://www.newzealandnow.govt.nz/living-in-nz/money-tax/nz-tax-system
[180] See 'Taxes', *Newzealand Now*,
https://www.newzealandnow.govt.nz/living-in-nz/money-tax/nz-tax-system

income[181] for the FY 2014-2015 stood at Rs 265,732.9 crores, while the revised estimate for 2015-2016 was pegged at Rs 299,051.24 crores and the budget estimate for 2016-2017 stands at Rs 353,173.68 crores. In each case, income tax revenue as a percentage of gross tax revenues stands at a little over 20 percent. Any proposal to revise the income tax rates is hence bound to have a significant impact on the country's tax revenues and this needs to be kept in mind.

The Nagpur based economic think-tank Arthakranti,[182] which has reportedly claimed credit for proposing the idea of demonetization to Prime Minister Modi, has proposed a complete abolition of all direct and indirect taxes levied by the Union Government, the various state governments and all local bodies across the country, with the exception of customs and import duties that function as international trade balancers. Instead, they propose a banking transactions tax (BTT) at the rate of 2 percent on all banking transactions, with the exception of cash withdrawals.

Given that demonetization is bound to bring a large number of the as yet excluded population into the formal banking system, they believe that the accruals from the banking transactions tax would compensate

---

[181] See 'Receipts Budget, 2016-2017',
http://indiabudget.nic.in/ub2016-17/rec/allrec.pdf
[182] See 'Banking Transaction Tax: After demonetisation, Arthakranti wants Narendra Modi to abolish Income Tax', November 18, 2016, *Artha Kranti,* India.com, http://www.arthakranti.org/news-events/238-banking-transaction-tax-after-demonetisation-arthakranti-wants-narendra-modi-to-abolish-income-tax

for the loss of income tax collections given the increased volume of transactions. An abolition of income tax would come as a big relief to the individual taxpayers, who would be left with a much larger discretionary income at their disposal and hence much improved purchasing power. This in turn will give a much needed push to economic activity and growth.

Banking transactions tax[183] as a concept is not new to the Indian fiscal system. The tax was introduced in 2005 by the earlier (UPA[184]) regime as a mechanism to trace black money. It was levied only on cash withdrawals of greater than Rs 50,000 (for individuals) and Rs 100,000 (for others) in a single working day from the non-savings accounts maintained with scheduled banks. The tax was subsequently withdrawn in 2009.

Given that BTT would be a flat, single-point tax to be levied by commercial banks on all bank transactions, it would be simple to implement and have practically zero compliance cost. With the numbers of those within the fold of the banking system expected to increase post demonetization, BTT is likely to generate the required tax revenue and have buoyancy besides. The negative fallout might be an attempt at bypassing the banking system, but, in

---

[183] See 'Govt abolishes banking transaction tax', April 1, 2009, *The Indian Express,* Agencies,
http://indianexpress.com/article/business/banking-and-finance/govt-abolishes-banking-transaction-tax/
[184] UPA stands for United Progressive Alliance. See
https://en.wikipedia.org/wiki/United_Progressive_Alliance

the aftermath of demonetization, it can be hoped that people would prefer not to transact in cash, wherever and whenever possible, in the light of their recent experiences. However, there exists the challenge of ensuring that the people newly entering the banking system remain within its fold. Simplifying banking procedures and improving the quality of and access to other support services should help achieve that.

Let us look at transaction numbers to understand how beneficial the BTT could be if implemented. For the month of October, 2016 alone, the total RTGS and NEFT transaction amounts across banks[185] stood at Rs 85,977.79 billion. A BTT on this at 2 percent would yield Rs 1,719.55 billion or Rs 171,955 crores. In FY 2016-2017, the budget estimates for gross tax revenue stands at Rs 1,630,887.88 crores. If one were to try to make a projection based on the total BTT estimate for NEFT and RTGS transactions alone based on October 2016 data, the annual total yield from BTT should compensate for the loss of revenue from all other direct taxes to the Union government and it would also be far easier and cost far less to implement and ensure compliance.

However, this step would require the various states of the Indian Union to buy into it, since it would be eliminating all other taxes that come under their purview. They would only receive a percentage of the Union government's net revenue from the BTT and

---

[185] See 'Bankwise Volumes in ECS/NEFT/RTGS/Mobile Transactions', *Reserve Bank of India*,
https://rbi.org.in/SCRIPTS/NEFTUserView.aspx?Id=102

the GST. In addition, it is essential to ensure that measures towards eliminating black money yield results and the banking system is expanded to ensure universal coverage. However, it would be prudent to exempt all pensions below a specified level and subsidy payments to those below the poverty line from BTT, even while ensuring that there are no leakages by not specifying any lower limits for BTT.

However, since BTT requires an extensive buy-in, an alternative method would be to raise the income tax exemption limit. The present exemption limit of Rs 2.5 lakhs is rather low. In my opinion, it inhibits the entrepreneurial drive and the incentive to make money. Coupled with the numerous exemptions, the transaction cost associated with administering such a system is enormous. Therefore, I am of the view that the income exemption limit may be enhanced to Rs 1,000,000/- from the coming financial year. A tax rate of 15 percent should be levied on all net incomes that fall above the specified limit. In the case of agricultural income alone, the exemption limit can be fixed at Rs 2,000,000. This will provide the necessary impetus to agriculture, while bringing into the tax net the larger farm holders and higher earning agriculturists.

Alongside, capital gains tax (long-term) should be removed and short-term capital gains should be coupled with regular income and taxed accordingly. If required, a nominal BTT of around 0.2 percent could be introduced as a test measure to compensate for any losses accruing from raising the exemption limit and rationalizing the tax rates. The benefits again would be huge savings in income tax administration, a more transparent tax system and an incentive to not hoard money.

The data[186] from the assessment year 2014-2015 indicates that a total of 48 million individuals were tax assesses, amounting to 3.81 percent of India's population. Of this, just over 1.33 million income-tax assesses declared an income of over Rs 10 lakh per year. Thus, just 2 percent of tax assesses will continue to remain in the tax bracket if the exemption limit were to be raised. However, a closer look reveals that, as per 2011-2012 data,[187] the assesses in the 10 lakhs plus income bracket contributed as much as 75 percent of the total income tax collected in terms of value. **That is why the suggestion to enhance the Income Tax exemption limit to Rs 10 lakhs has been made.** Therefore, given the above, increasing the exemption limit is not expected to have the effect of turning over the collection figures altogether. So far as corporate income tax goes, the current tax rate of 30 percent can be lowered[188] to 20 percent without allowing for any deductions.

---

[186] See 'Only 3.81% Indians pay Income Tax; Maharashtra, Delhi pay 53% of the total', May 3, 2016, *First Post*, IndiaSpend, http://googleweblight.com/?lite_url=http%3A%2F%2Fm.firstpost.c om%2Fbusiness%2Fonly-3-81-indians-pay-income-tax-maharashtra-delhi-pay-53-2761510.html&ei=mlZek-sE&lc=en-IN&s=1&m=908&host=www.google.co.in&ts=1480263361&sig=A F9NedmGzO3gZXq2D9OVbEDugulKuxRE-w
[187] See 'Income Taxes paid by Indians [Overview, Numbers & Graphs]', May 1, 2012, *Trak.in*, Arun Prabhudesai, http://trak.in/tags/business/2012/04/30/income-taxes-paid-indians-overview-numbers-graphs/
[188] The net rate of tax paid by corporates is reported to be 23% - See 'To lessen demonetisation pain: Tax sops in Budget', December 05,

The Cinderella Notes

At this point in time, it would be difficult to make exact projections on yield or shortfall in tax revenues as a result of such changes to the tax structure. Much like the demonetization move, this would have to be a leap of faith, a trial run to a degree, before we are able to arrive at an optimal taxation system that yields sufficient revenue to lubricate the public expenditure system even as it leaves the citizens happy, unburdened, hassle-free and willing to loosen their purse strings sufficiently to keep the economy growing at a decent pace.

While on the subject of tax reforms as a means to combat black money, the issue of unaccounted income stashed away in offshore accounts needs to be considered as well. Many of the opponents to the demonetization move have criticized it on the grounds that it addresses only the negligible cash component of the black money in circulation within the country, while turning a blind eye to the black money converted to assets like real estate, gold or stock and most importantly, cash deposits in offshore accounts.

Given that real estate constitutes about a tenth of the Indian economy, the black money floating around in real estate is estimated to be many times higher[189] than the riches stashed away in offshore accounts.

2016, *Rediff.com*, Dilasha Seth and Arup Roy Choudhury, Business Standard, http://m.rediff.com/business/report/to-lessen-demonetisation-pain-tax-sops-in-budget/20161205.htm

[189] See 'Real estate: An industry built on black money', December 05, 2014, *Rediff.com*, Bhupesh Bhandari, http://www.rediff.com/money/report/pix-column-real-estate-an-industry-built-on-black-money/20141205.htm

The Cinderella Notes

One can only hope that rationalization of taxes on the acquisition of property and also personal income tax and corporate tax rates will prove as a natural deterrent to the real estate sector continuing to be the receptacle of black money that it currently is.

On the matter of repatriating black money lying in offshore accounts, the government is faced with a formidable task and significant legal wrangling given that it also involves the framework of the prevailing laws of those countries where the monies lie.

According to a Bank of Italy estimate, Indians[190] have stashed away $152-$181 billion in offshore foreign bank accounts. Although India has had to depend on revelations like the Panama Papers expose until now for access to data, the country has signed agreements with several OECD[191] member countries for automatic flow of information, which will come into effect from January, 2017. Swiss banks[192] have also agreed to share information on Indian account holders from September, 2019, following a joint declaration signed between the two countries. A revised tax treaty was signed recently with

---

[190] See 'Baiting the big fish', October 6, 2016, *India Today*, Shweta Punj, http://indiatoday.intoday.in/story/black-money-tax-income-tax-modi-government-income-disclosure-scheme/1/781362.html
[191] The Organisation for Economic Co-operation and Development (OECD) (French: *Organisation de coopération et de développement économiques, OCDE*) is an intergovernmental economic organisation with 35 member countries, founded in 1961 to stimulate economic progress and world trade.
[192] See 'Swiss Banks to share info on Indian A/C holders', November 22, 2016, *The Times of India*, PTI, http://timesofindia.indiatimes.com/india/Swiss-Banks-to-share-info-on-Indian-A/C-holders-from-Sept-2019/articleshow/55562640.cms

Mauritius[193] to enable the government to tax capital gains on investments routed through the island nation, one of the preferred tax havens of Indian investors. India has signed a DTAA (Double Taxation Avoidance Agreement)[194] with 88 countries, including most major countries such as the United States, the United Kingdom, Australia and France. Mauritius, Cyprus and Singapore were the only three countries where the agreement was earlier not in force. As of 2016, the agreements with both Mauritius and Cyprus have been renegotiated and signed, while it is hoped that the treaty with Singapore[195] will be signed before the end of the fiscal period. All of these come as huge jolts to Indian investors hoping to avoid paying tax on income from capital gains.

The provisions of the Prevention of Money Laundering Act[196] (PMLA) and FEMA[197] (Foreign

---

[193] See 'Revised Indo-Mauritius tax treaty to curb tax evasion: Finance Ministry', August 29, 2016, *The Economic Times*, PTI, http://economictimes.indiatimes.com/news/economy/policy/revised-indo-mauritius-tax-treaty-to-curb-tax-evasion-finance-ministry/articleshow/53912921.cms
[194] See 'All you wanted to know about...DTAA', May 16, 2016, Business Line, Parvatha Vardhini.C, http://www.thehindubusinessline.com/opinion/columns/all-you-wanted-to-know-aboutdtaa/article8607732.ece
[195] See 'India hopeful of signing new tax treaty with Singapore by this fiscal end', May 16, 2016, *The Hindu Business Line*, Surabhi, http://www.thehindubusinessline.com/economy/policy/india-hopeful-of-signing-new-tax-treaty-with-singapore-by-this-fiscal-end/article8607967.ece
[196] See 'Prevention of Money Laundering Act, 2002', http://finmin.nic.in/law/moneylaunderingact.pdf

Exchange Management Act) were amended under the Undisclosed Foreign Income and Assets (Imposition of Tax) Bill,[198] 2015, to ensure that, in the event of undisclosed assets held by a person abroad not being attachable, assets of equivalent value held by such a person in India would be confiscated. The bill proposed that a flat tax rate of 30 percent, without allowing for any of the exemptions permitted under the Income Tax Act would be applied on all foreign income. An enhanced punishment including imprisonment for between 3-10 years and a penalty of three times the tax amount, amounting to 90 percent of the undisclosed income was also proposed on any wilful non-disclosure or tax evasion. A one-time compliance window was also announced between June and September, 2015, for Indian citizens to declare information on all previously undisclosed assets, which would be taxed at a flat 30 percent along with a penalty of 100 percent of the tax amount. The rate of taxation in effect was 60 percent of the undisclosed income. During the compliance period, the disclosures would not attract the provisions of FEMA or PMLA.

The scheme was not particularly successful, netting only Rs 3770 crores[199] in income disclosures with a

---

[197] See 'Foreign Exchange Management Act, 1999', Income Tax Department, http://www.incometaxindia.gov.in/pages/acts/foreign-exchange-management-act.aspx

[198] See 'The Undisclosed Foreign Income and Assets (Imposition of Tax) Bill, 2015', as Introduced In Lok Sabha, http://www.incometaxindia.gov.in/Documents/Undisclosed-Foreign-Income-Bill-2015.pdf

[199] See 'Why black money scheme was a superflop, and what Modi can do to redeem it', October 3, 2015, *First Post*, R Jagannathan,

60 percent tax plus penalty to be levied on them. The figure cannot reflect more than a miniscule portion of the cash and assets held abroad.

Clearly, there is a need for better incentives if the country is to be successful in repatriating funds and assets from abroad. While the law has been sufficiently armed to prosecute them, it will only end up being a long drawn out process and might not yield the results hoped for. Instead, if compliance can be achieved voluntarily, by providing sufficient incentives for them to disclose their foreign holdings and bring them back to the country, it would do the economy far greater good. Like the recently proposed deposit of 25 percent of undisclosed income into a designated welfare scheme, a similar or the same fund could be identified for the deposit of foreign cash reserves over and above the applicable tax rate. Rather than imposing heavy penalties, a lock-in period of a few years might encourage the individual to disclose his assets, given that he has the hope of regaining use of them at some future point, as opposed to completely losing the use of them in the form of stiff penalties.

Yet another reform that has been discussed is the adoption of a something similar to the American IRS (Internal Revenue Service) scheme. The success of the IRS[200] in attracting foreign capital of Americans (back) into the United States needs commendation.

http://www.firstpost.com/business/why-the-black-money-scheme-was-a-superflop-and-what-modi-can-do-to-redeem-it-2452626.html
[200] See appendix 7.

The Cinderella Notes

The system basically allows a country to tax the income and wealth of all its citizens, irrespective of where it originates from. Once again, issues such as transparency and sharing of data and information are crucial to the success of such a measure.

The larger point to be underlined here is that the stick alone cannot work, carrots are needed too and they must be sufficiently designed so that they encourage the return of foreign capital back to India in a voluntary manner. Engaging in legal battles with institutions in overseas countries can become counter productive and a waste of time and money.

Overall, the proposed restructuring of the tax system should be made attractive enough to the taxpayer to want to retain his capital within the country, rather than go to the trouble of transferring and maintaining it in offshore accounts.

Apart from structural reforms, compliance windows and simplifying tax procedures, the other critical aspect that needs addressing, with respect to influencing attitudinal change, is the cost benefit analysis to the taxpayer. By benefit, I do not refer to personal benefit alone but benefit to the larger society. If the taxpayer sees the tax he pays yield dividend in the form of better public health, education, transport and other infrastructure, he might start feeling more invested in the process of nation building. If, however, he perceives no change in the quality of public infrastructure and sees the bulk of his tax money going towards wasteful and extravagant government expenditure, he would feel increasingly resentful of the taxation process.

It is, therefore, imperative to trim the fat from government expenditure, to make it a mean and lean machine that delivers true cost benefits to the exchequer. After having willingly borne the pain of demonetization, the taxpayer will certainly want to see the lawmakers and bureaucrats responding by practicing a certain austerity in the use of public money and diverting all public resources to projects intended for public good.

Also, it is imperative that the government machinery starts recognizing that it is accountable to the taxpayer, whose tax money is what keeps it lubricated and running. The attitude of policy makers, bureaucrats and other government staff also needs to change towards the taxpayer and he needs to be accorded the respect he deserves in his interactions with the State. He must not be pushed around or trifled with and he must not be expected to pay bribes and commissions to get work done within the government. It would be adding insult to injury if, after willingly participating in the war against corruption and black money, he is forced to bribe his way through the government's administrative labyrinth to get his license, permits or even his pension/dues—all this even after following due process.

From posing a conundrum, the taxation system needs to evolve into a more just, compassionate and simple process that the taxpayer is happily willing to

The Cinderella Notes

participate in, simply because he perceives a palpable difference on the ground that convinces him that there is a point to it after all, one of larger good!

CHAPTER 6

Building Blocks

'Demonetisation will hurt GDP in the short run[201]'
'Demonetisation will hit agriculture, informal sector workers the most: Study[202]'
'Startups see decline in business after demonetisation: Survey[203]'
'Over 80 percent don't mind inconvenience of demonetisation, says C-Voter poll[204]'

Shared above are samples of Indian newspaper headlines from the days that followed

---

[201] See 'Demonetisation will hurt GDP in the short run', November 25, 2016, *The Hindu Business Line*, Our Bureau,
http://www.thehindubusinessline.com/money-and-banking/demonetisation-to-have-negative-impact-on-growth-in-short-run-fitch/article9386078.ece
[202] See 'Demonetisation will hit agriculture, informal sector workers the most: Study', November 15, 2016, First Post, Abhishek Waghmare, http://www.firstpost.com/india/demonetisation-will-hit-agriculture-informal-sector-workers-the-most-study-3106004.html
[203] See 'Startups see decline in business after demonetisation: Survey', November 23, 2016, *The Economic Times*, IANS,
http://economictimes.indiatimes.com/small-biz/startups/startups-see-decline-in-business-after-demonetisation-survey/articleshow/55580466.cms
[204] See 'Over 80 percent don't mind inconvenience of demonetisation, says C-Voter poll', November 23, 2016, *The Times of India*, http://timesofindia.indiatimes.com/india/Over-80-percent-dont-mind-inconvenience-of-demonetisation-says-C-Voter-poll/articleshow/55566700.cms

demonetization. It is fairly obvious that the last one appears not quite congruent with the rest. Despite the obvious suffering and the projected economic loss, a significant majority seemed to have expressed their support for the move. It would, of course, be easy for opponents to dismiss the sample as non-representational or pick other flaws in the survey technique. The fact remains that the survey was conducted by one of the better polling agencies in the country.

What is the one compelling reason that makes many Indians continue to support the demonetization move despite the rather gloomy predictions about the future of the Indian economy? Rising above the prism of political biases, if one were to put his finger on one single compelling reason, I would say that it is *hope*. The man on the streets is no economist, nor is he a fool. He is hardly oblivious to the problems and the pains that the decision has imposed on him; he is suffering through them after all. Yet, he looks beyond the immediate in hope; a hope that this might just be that kick in the backside badly needed by an exploitative system mired in corruption for decades. In addition, there is possibly a certain perverse pleasure that he derives at the thought of the rich and mighty, grown richer and more powerful with time, not being so invincible anymore.

He sees them edgy and restless, much like the proverbial cat on the hot tin roof; he hears reports of large amounts of cash dumped into river waters and garbage bins; he hears of the rich negotiating with the poor to save their skins for a price; he hears of the

The Cinderella Notes

Income Tax raids on the rich and mighty. And he feels that perhaps the status quo will soon be shaken up. Maybe he will suffer in the immediate future but maybe, just maybe, this is the beginning of something better after all!

A cynic might dismiss this hope as an illusion, since it might not be grounded in hard fact, but I see this hope as that all important glue that holds together the building blocks of a nation, of an economy. It is this hope that will stir up enterprise, innovation, hard work and commitment. Without this hope, the common man will not have the will to try to beat a system where the odds are loaded against him. After years of inertia, of seeing nothing really changing, suddenly everything appears in a flux and there is an almighty churning, not unlike the mythical churning of the ocean that first yielded venom. He believes that if he is stoic in adversity, maybe the venom will be followed by great good. We Indians are a people of faith, after all!

If a society, an economy, loses this hope of survival and progress, then all is lost. It is crucial for this hope to be kept alive, to be kindled so the common man feels invested in the process, so that he contributes to it with all his might and spirit.

Having inspired hope, it is now the turn of the government to ensure that it is not belied. That people are rewarded for their faith, for the forbearance they have displayed in adversity, with true and equitable economic growth, and the economy derives all the benefits that the trigger of demonetization has the potential to yield.

The first step towards realizing the hope of the common man is providing an impetus for growth. That impetus can only come from building a strong infrastructural base. The building blocks need to be sturdy and well-aligned if the structure of the economy is to be stable enough to serve the needs of its population.

The three building blocks that form the base on which the Indian economy rests are agriculture and allied sectors, manufacturing and services. While agriculture is the mainstay of the rural economy, the industries and the services sectors are a more urban and peri-urban phenomena.

Even as demonetization appears to have taken the wind out of the sails of the economy it has also succeeded in highlighting certain lacunae in each of these core sectors. It is now time for all these lacunae to be addressed and the core capacity of these sectors improved/strengthened to increase their productivity/output. Tremendous opportunity to revive the economy lies therein and it needs to be grabbed and exploited, if we are to prevent the economy from falling into recession as a result of the near-term consequences of the cash crunch post demonetization.

In order to gain perspective on ways forward in re-energizing the economy, it would be beneficial to take a detailed look at the three major components that form the base of the Indian economy.

Agriculture: Agriculture in India is largely dependent on the vagaries of nature, in the absence of proper irrigation facilities. Crop failure is literally the curse of death for farmers across the country, particularly in Maharashtra, Karnataka, Madhya Pradesh and Chhattisgarh among others. Faced with mounting debts and no means to repay the same because of a failed monsoon, farmers often choose the 'release of death over the misery of living'. And for those who continue living, the Damocles sword in the form of a failed monsoon and ensuing crop failure is always hanging over their heads.

According to World Bank data,[205] the contribution of agriculture to India's GDP fell from 26.3 percent in 1995 to 17.4 percent in 2014. In terms of total employment, the sector's intake[206] fell from 61 percent in 1994 to 51 percent in 2010. Indeed, a worrying fall that needs to be heeded as a working signal, given the consequent implications for food security in the medium and longer term. Yet another cause for concern is that, despite the fall in the sector's share of the GDP, under 58 percent of the rural households are said to depend[207] on agriculture as their principal means of livelihood.

---

[205] See 'Agriculture, value added (% of GDP)', *The World Bank*, http://data.worldbank.org/indicator/NV.AGR.TOTL.ZS
[206] See 'Employment in agriculture (% of total employment)', *The World Bank*, http://data.worldbank.org/indicator/SL.AGR.EMPL.ZS
[207] See 'Indian Agriculture Industry: an overview', *India Brand Equity Foundation (IBEF)*, http://www.ibef.org/industry/agriculture-

The Cinderella Notes

The challenging scenario that reportedly unfolded in the agricultural and allied sectors, and the rural economy largely dependent on them, is of course, directly attributable to the fact that cash has been their primary mode of transaction. Farmers and small traders prefer to deal in cash and most village markets/mandis operate on cash, since the transaction costs ensuing from engaging with the formal banking sector are perceived as too high by the farmers. So, when the SBN component of their cash holdings ceased to be legal tender on the midnight of November 8, it proved to be a double whammy. Not only had a significant portion of the cash reserves suddenly become non-fungible, but there was also the difficulty of access in exchanging the demonetized currency. There was a delay in the newly minted currency reaching rural branches, on account of the distance from the RBI state currency chests and ease of overall access.

The timing of the announcement also served to compound the miseries of the agricultural sector. Crops from the *kharif* season had been harvested and were ready for transportation and sale at the markets and the farmers were getting ready to sow the *rabi* crop when the announcement came. There were media reports[208] of wholesale markets being badly

---

india.aspx according to which the figure is 58%. Also see 'Only 40 per cent of rural households dependent on farming as main income source: NSSO', December 22, 2014, *Indian Express*, Harish Damodaran,http://indianexpress.com/article/business/business-others/theres-less-of-krishi-in-bharat-now/

[208] See 'Demonetisation has left India's food markets frozen – and the future looks tense', November 18, 2016, *Scroll.in*, M Rajshekhar,

disrupted by the absence of cash and the farmers finding no takers for their produce or being forced to suffer losses by selling at low prices.

There were also reported issues of lack of proper warehousing and storage facilities resulting in perishable commodities being left to rot. Movement of produce to the markets was also affected with the payment of toll fees[209] becoming a problem. The produce subsequently ended up being stranded at different points with the truckers short of cash to pay toll fees and other charges. Wage labour was not available at the markets to offload the produce from the trucks since there was no cash available to pay their wages. And even in the retail markets, sales dipped considerably since people did not have sufficient cash in hand to pay the small vendors, who had no means of accepting any other mode of payment but cash. With a large portion of the cash in their hands rendered non-fungible, the farmers had no money to buy seeds[210] for the new season.

Abhishek Dey, http://scroll.in/article/821834/demonetisation-has-left-indias-food-markets-frozen-and-the-future-looks-tense

[209] The government subsequently ordered for the toll charges at highways to be waived up to December 2, 2016—See 'Toll waiver on national highways extended till 2 December: government', November 24, 2016, *Livemint*, Manasi,

Lohumi,http://www.livemint.com/Politics/C3JAk8Sps59Wp0551e41VI/Toll-waiver-on-National-Highways-extended-till-2-December.html

[210] The government subsequently permitted farmers to use the SBNs to buy seeds from notified outlets.

See 'Farmers can now use old Rs 500 notes to buy seeds', November 21, 2016, *Indian Express*, Express Web Desk,

http://indianexpress.com/article/business/economy/farmers-seeds-old-rs-500-notes-demonetisation-4387350/

Agricultural wage labour, like in the case of plantations, was affected since labourers could not be paid owing to the cash crunch.

The district credit co-operatives (DCCBs), with whom the majority of the farmers hold their accounts, were initially permitted to accept deposits of the SBNs (but no exchange), the RBI[211] soon after imposed a ban on their accepting SBNs under any circumstances. DCCB managements are reportedly dominated by political forces[212] and it was feared that permitting them to participate in the exchange/deposit process could facilitate money laundering.[213]

With respect to access to formal financial services, the farmers are in a rather unique situation that keeps them oscillating between being excluded and included within the fold of the banking sector[214]. Like pointed out earlier, many of them do hold accounts with the DCCBs but the present credit and insurance schemes are often themselves reason for alienating the farmers from accessing formal financial

---

[211] See 'Applicability of the Scheme to DCCBs', November 14, 2016, *Reserve Bank of India,*
https://rbi.org.in/Scripts/BS_CircularIndexDisplay.aspx?Id=10707
[212] See 'Why govt stopped co-op banks from changing 500/1,000 notes', November 18, 2016, *Rediff.com,* A Ganesh Nadar,
http://www.rediff.com/business/report/why-govt-stopped-co-op-banks-from-changing-5001000-notes/20161118.htm
[213] See 'Kerala will bear the biggest brunt of demonetisation: Cooperative banks gasping for breath', Nov 15, 2016, First Post, G Pramod Kumar, http://www.firstpost.com/india/kerala-will-bear-the-biggest-brunt-of-demonetisation-cooperative-banks-gasping-for-breath-3106408.html

services. This is the case as the terms and conditions under which these schemes operate are loaded in favour of those offering them as opposed to the beneficiaries. For example, sugar factories are the source of the setts[215] that sugarcane farmers use for cultivation of the crop. Banks normally provide them credit at the time of issue of setts, with the loans to be repaid after harvest and sale of the produce. However, there is always the danger of these 'setts' being bad, not germinating sufficiently and thereby reducing overall yield. The liability of the farmer remains unchanged even then and neither the factory nor the bank, share in such risk. The onus to repay is on the farmer, irrespective of the quality of the 'setts'[216] and their potential yield.

Similarly, insurance schemes make for so many exemptions that, more often, the farmer's claims are either rejected outright or so vastly reduced as to be rendered inconsequential.

Under the circumstances, when a farmer is unable to repay a loan, he automatically steers clear of his bank and thereafter gets excluded from the banking system. Post demonetization, there were stories of several farmers not wanting to go to banks to deposit or exchange their SBNs since they were worried that

---

[215] Stem cuttings or sections of the stalks called 'setts' or seed pieces propagate sugarcane.
[216] In many situations, the gap filling of sugarcane fields, done for low level of germination of 'setts', is done by the farmer at the instance of the sugar factory/bank. The cost is however borne only by the farmer.

the banks might adjust what little money they had against their previously overdue loans.[217]

From the above scenarios, it becomes abundantly clear that while it is important to improve the access of farmers to financial services and products to enable them to make the shift from a predominantly cash based (informal) to a formal economy, it is not the cure to all that ails the agricultural sector and the rural economy at large. In this context, and keeping in mind the various problems that the demonetization process has helped underline as key issues, I would like to suggest the following as important elements for a more sweeping structural change (at sufficient scale[218]) that could yield larger benefits to the agriculture sector.

Repositioning agriculture and rural life—This calls for priority focus on access to finance in agriculture in terms of investment credit, risk mitigation products and finance for infrastructure, including watershed, extension services, quality inputs and standardisation.

Promoting innovation, competitiveness and growth of agribusiness—Competition enhancing finance for players in various agriculture supply chains (mainly, middle level) and especially for other kinds of intermediaries (like producer organisations). This

---

[217] See 'Demonetisation Has Wrecked Farmers', November 28, 2016, *The Wire*, Jaideep Hardikar, http://thewire.in/83072/demonetisation-has-wrecked-farmers/

[218] India is a great country for pilots and many innovative projects are essentially in the pilot testing mode but scale is very critical to achieve medium and long term impact.

apart, there could be specialised financial arrangements for re-structuring of such supply chains and similar systems. Improving access to new markets and providing information on prevailing commodity rates are also critical inputs here.

Strengthening agricultural health and food safety systems—It is critical to do this in terms of inputs, processes and infrastructure and ensure that various standards are adhered to. Finance for infrastructure is important here and offers a great opportunity.

Introducing appropriate technology and innovation for modernisation of agriculture and rural life—Again, innovative financial products can play a major role here in bringing technologies from lab to land in a successful manner and facilitating their wider adoption by small producers and farmers.

Strengthening existing agricultural infrastructure— Enhancing the staying and bargaining power of small and marginal farmers is going to be very critical. Thus, finance for reducing vulnerability and risks of small producers would be most useful and this alone will enable them to participate fully as stakeholders and ensure that they get their due. This would include a range of post-harvest financing arrangements, including warehouse receipts, again at sufficient scale all across the country. Also, storage and warehousing infrastructure needs to be improved everywhere to invest farmers with bargaining power and the strength to hold out for better prices. Setting up allied industries that offer value addition to agricultural produce, with a view to increasing their use and shelf-life, will also serve their cause well.

Manufacturing: The industrial[219] sector's contribution to GDP stood at 24.2 percent for the year 2014, of which around 17 percent came from manufacturing.[220] Around 12 percent of the country's workforce[221] is employed by this sector.

The Make in India[222] initiative was launched in 2014 with a view to increasing the capacity of the country's industrial and manufacturing sector, to attract FDI (Foreign Direct Investment) flow into the sector and thereby improve the sector's contribution to the GDP as well as to employment generation. It was estimated[223] that the manufacturing sector had the potential to account for 25-30 percent of the

---

[219] See 'Sector-wise contribution of GDP of India', July 08, 2015, *Statistics Times,* Planning Commission, Government of India, http://statisticstimes.com/economy/sectorwise-gdp-contribution-of-india.php
[220] See 'Manufacturing sector's contribution to GDP will increase', October 10, 2015, *The Hindu,* R Krishnamoorthy, http://www.thehindu.com/news/national/tamil-nadu/manufacturing-sectors-contribution-to-gdp-will-increase/article7745387.ece
[221] See 'Manufacturing', *Confederation of Indian Industry (CII),* http://www.cii.in/sectors.aspx?enc=prvePUj2bdMtgTmvPwvisYH+5EnGjyGXO9hLECvTuNsfVm32+poFSr33jmZ/rN+5
[222] Make in India is an initiative launched by the Government of India to encourage multi-national, as well as national companies to manufacture their products in India.
[223] See 'Manufacturing', October, 2016, *India in business,* Ministry of External Affairs, Govt. of India, Economic Diplomacy Division, http://indiainbusiness.nic.in/newdesign/index.php?param=industryservices_landing/411/2

country's GDP and create up to 90 million domestic jobs by 2025.

An economic survey places the increase in FDI[224] between October 2014 and June 2015 at 40 percent. While this appears creditable, the flip side of capital outflow also needs to be considered. Statistics[225] provided by OECD[226] indicate that, during the period 2006 to 2012, FDI outflow was around $103.30 billion, while inflow was just over double that number ($212.70 billion). In 2014, while India's GDP grew by around 5 percent, overseas FDI (OFDI) from India likewise increased by almost 8 per cent, most of it in the form of mergers and acquisitions.

A number of these investments, especially in the areas of consumer goods industries and services, are routed through offshore centres like Singapore, Mauritius, the Netherlands, Cyprus and the British Virgin Islands; countries that boast of friendly taxation regimes coupled with legal statuses that prove to be beneficial for corporations and thus, are

---

[224] See 'FDI inflows rise 40% on Make in India initiative: Economic Survey', February 27 2016, *Livemint*, Shine Jacob,
http://www.livemint.com/Politics/sYFaCzUi4paE9UCajwYjuO/F DI-inflows-rise-40-on-Make-in-India-initiative-Economic-S.html
[225] See 'Indian direct investment', June 29, 2015, *The Indian Express*, Christophe Jaffrelot,
http://indianexpress.com/article/opinion/columns/indian-direct-investment/
[226] The Organisation for Economic Co-operation and Development (OECD) (French: *Organisation de coopération et de développement économiques, OCDE*) is an intergovernmental economic organisation with 35 member countries, founded in 1960 to stimulate economic progress and world trade.

more often motivated by financial calculations. There is a significant amount of OFDI that flows into real estate as well.

While many of these transactions might be perfectly above board, the intent of benefitting from friendly taxation regimes is not quite in the interests of the country. This is especially because of the need in the country for huge capital outlay for infrastructure development and employment generation.

If demonetization is followed by restructuring of the tax laws (as already discussed in the earlier Chapter 5), alongside rooting out corruption, simplifying procedures (for permits and licenses by cutting through the bureaucratic red tape) to enhance ease of doing business and enabling systems to be more encouraging of enterprises, India might be better placed to retain domestic capital even as the country works hard at wooing foreign investments. We might also be able to succeed in the repatriation of the black money stashed in offshore accounts. This could again serve India's growing capital needs in a big way but needs to be approached in a mature and practical manner. The disappearance of capital to foreign shores through tax havens like Panama must be curbed at all costs.

In the context of Make in India, a key area that has reportedly suffered serious impact in the wake of demonetization is the MSME (Micro, Small and

Medium Enterprises) sector. As per latest figures,[227] the sector consists of 36 million units, provides employment to over 80 million persons, and contributes about 8 percent to GDP besides 45 percent to the total manufacturing output and 40 percent to the exports through its more than 6000 products. Out of the 36 million units, 34.6 million[228] are unregistered. As high as 55 percent of these unregistered units are part of the rural economy.

With the rural economy transacting predominantly in cash, an estimated 55 percent of the total unregistered MSMEs[229], all located in the villages, reportedly bore the brunt of the demonetization impact. While the impact should not have been as severe in the urban economy, especially given the better access to banking facilities (both qualitatively and quantitatively), the size of the urban MSME units and value of their cash transactions—both of which dictated a larger use of cash in the city based MSMEs as well—caused them to suffer to a degree as well.

---

[227] See 'MSME At A Glance 2016', January 2016, *Ministry of Micro, Small & Medium Enterprises*, Government of India,
http://msme.gov.in/WriteReadData/ebook/MSME_at_a_GLANCE_2016_Final.pdf
[228] See 'Annual Report 2015-16', *Ministry of Micro, Small and Medium Enterprises*, Government of India,
http://msme.gov.in/WriteReadData/DocumentFile/MEME%20ANNUAL%20REPORT%202015-16%20ENG.pdf
[229] See 'Demonetisation effect: Unbanked villages, small businesses badly hit as currency crisis continues', November 21, 2016, The Indian Express, Anil Sasi, P. Vaidyanathan Iyer,
http://indianexpress.com/article/business/economy/demonetisation-effect-unbanked-villages-small-businesses-badly-hit-as-currency-crisis-continues-4385176/

Thus, MSMEs in both rural and urban areas, with their cash reserves reportedly rendered non-fungible for the most part, were impacted by the cash crunch in terms of accessing raw material and goods in wholesale markets. Their sales were just as severely impacted since their clientele mostly paid in cash too. Sales and orders, in the case of service oriented MSMEs, dipped dangerously and the market research firm Ambit Capital[230] indicated that there would be a significant increase in NPAs (non-performing assets) from the MSME sector. There was also the fear of a number of MSMEs failing and shutting down or shrinking in size—both of which would surely lead to loss of jobs.

The benefit of demonetization has been that a large majority of the MSMEs that are part of the informal economy have been integrated with the formal economy, at least temporarily. The question of whether they will continue to remain integrated is one that only time can answer. However, given the experience of demonetization and its consequences, there is a good chance that there would be an attitudinal and a behavioural change to a large extent. Small manufacturers, vendors and service providers might want to continue with banking/digital transactions owing to the fear of losing business in the absence of cash and also because of the huge impetus the government is trying to give to the creation of a relatively cash-free economy. These

---

[230] See 'Demonetisation May Increase NPAs From SME Sector: Ambit Capital', November 15, 2016, *NDTV*, http://www.ndtv.com/video/business/news/demonetisation-may-increase-npas-from-sme-sector-ambit-capital-438763

messages need to be reinforced positively by the government and sufficient infrastructure and incentives provided for MSMEs to continue transacting with the formal financial institutions that they are coming into contact with, especially because of the demonetization.

The MSMEs would also hugely benefit from improved and increased access to the "right kind"[231] of formal financial services, which will help them expand their operations, increase economies of scale and access larger and better markets for their products.

The MSMEs would also benefit from some degree of marketing support. For one, a digital marketplace could be created for MSMEs to showcase their range of products/services. They could be categorized on the basis of the nature of product/service offered. The recently proposed initiative[232] of the government of India (which seeks to build a public procurement

---

[231] Inappropriate financial services cause more harm than good as the Indian microfinance and financial inclusion experience suggests. Please see Appendix 8 for the case of the sugarcane farmer, who often gets excluded because of the credit schemes in vogue. Also, credit for MSME's has to include investment credit, working capital, risk mitigation and vulnerability reducing financial products and post production/harvest financial products that reduce risks arising from market imperfections in the raw material, intermediate goods and final products (goods and services) markets and enhance the staying and bargaining power of the small MSME producers. Please see appendix 6 for lessons from the Indian microfinance experience.
[232] See 'Modi to 'Amazonize' $400 billion in state bids across India', December 01, 2016, *The Economic Times*, Archana Chaudhary, http://economictimes.indiatimes.com/news/economy/policy/modi-to-amazonize-400-billion-in-state-bids-across-india/articleshow/55716822.cms

portal on the lines of the Amazon e-marketplace) would be ideally suited and the suggested MSME products/services platform can be integrated with the same. And at least 50 percent of the government procurement could be linked to MSMEs, of which 25 percent can be mandatorily kept for women led MSMEs. Other countries, especially in the Commonwealth, have successfully earmarked such quotas for MSMEs and contributed to the overall growth of the MSME sector. Without a doubt, a strong MSME sector should go a long way towards contributing to a vibrant "Make in India" program.

Services: The services sector is the single largest contributor to India's GDP, with the figure[233] touching about 64 percent in 2015-2016. As per the NSSO (National Sample Survey Office) survey figures for 2011-2012, 82.7 percent of India's workforce are employed in the unorganized sector,[234] with more than 50 percent[235] comprising agricultural labour. MSMEs[236] employ almost 40 percent of the

---

[233] See 'Services Sector', July, 2016, *India in Business*, Ministry of External Affairs, Govt. of India, Economic Diplomacy Division, http://indiainbusiness.nic.in/newdesign/index.php?param=advantage/169

[234] See 'Over 47 crore workforce in country: NSSO', July 23, 2014, *The Economic Times*, PTI, http://articles.economictimes.indiatimes.com/2014-07-23/news/51932175_1_unorganised-sector-national-sample-survey-office-central-public-sector-enterprises

[235] See 'Unorganised labour force in India', *Vikaspedia*, Ministry of Labour and Employment, http://vikaspedia.in/social-welfare/unorganised-sector-1/categories-of-unorganised-labour-force

[236] See 'SME contribution to employment increased threefold', March 10, 2015, *SME Times*, SME Times News Bureau, http://www.smetimes.in/smetimes/news/top-

workforce, much of them again in the category of unorganized labour. This leaves close to 10 percent to be employed in the services sector, where again the percentage in the informal economy is huge.

Given the migrant nature of the unorganized labour population, whether in agriculture, construction, manufacturing industry and the like, bringing them into the folds of a formal financial system again presents a challenge. However, linking of Aadhar cards to payments and also the prevalence of core[237] or anywhere banking helps resolve some of the issues that this poses.

While demonetization has thrown life out of gear for the unorganized labour, it has also created an opportunity to bring their contribution to the country's GDP into official reckoning. In other words, there is a unique opportunity to recognize the hitherto ignored contribution of—the manpower employed in—the informal sector to the economy and thereafter, commensurately reward them with access to better opportunities in finance, markets, health care, pensions and all other aspects that can improve the overall quality of their life.

Also, given the huge volume of transactions present, there is a great opportunity for the formal

---

stories/2015/Mar/10/sme-contribution-to-employment-increased-threefold632024.html

[237] Core banking is a banking service provided by a group of networked bank branches where customers may access their bank accounts and perform basic transactions from any of the member branch offices.

financial/digital service providers to expand their outreach and client base. This will enable the informal economy to gain increased access to financial services, to be able to expand and strengthen their business operations and further improve their contribution to the formal economy and the country's GDP.

Apart from bringing them into the purview of the formal financial system to ensure timely and equitable payment of wages, the government would be benefited by creating an **online database of unorganized unskilled/semi-skilled labour** across the country. An initiative on these lines is already on the cards with Prime Minister Narendra Modi's government launching an online employment portal[238] in June, 2015.

This initiative can be expanded as it provides a great opportunity to aggregate and organize unorganized labour (from several sectors) through a special drive that will connect the labourers to potential employers seeking their services. I would even suggest that a statutory body be created (association of unorganized labour) and the labourers assigned fair stakes in it so that all other benefits like insurance, medical and retirement benefits can be provided to them. Such a body would also go a long way towards eliminating exploitation by middlemen and agents, who take hefty cuts/commissions to help these (informal sector) workers find jobs. This would also contribute

---

[238]Govt launches online employment portal, Jun 16 2015, *Live Mint*, http://www.livemint.com/Politics/HSSF33E2C0F8JOfPrLWPnJ/Govt-launches-job-portal-for-MSME-sector.html

immensely in helping to streamline the informal sector by facilitating the creation of better working and living conditions for the workers who are a part of it.

For example, as with construction projects that are issued completion certificates based on their adherence to parameters such as planning and safety norms, a certification mark may be created and accorded to projects/workplaces to indicate their degree of compliance with labour welfare measures, including provision of equitable pay and adherence to safety standards. This is just an example and several similar such initiatives could be considered and implemented, as per the needs and requirements of different sub-sectors.[239]

Furthermore, potential employers may also register their requirements online and based on the geographic location, potential service providers would be alerted to upcoming job opportunities. This will facilitate the matching of demand and supply between informal and unorganized sector workers and their potential employers. And once such a database becomes available and in use, financial services including remittances, emergency loans and the like can be provided by the formal financial sector based on the track record of work observed in the database. The model could be much the same as what Uber/ Ola Cabs use, where jobs are assigned to skilled labour in the database depending on

---

[239] By different sub-sectors, I am talking of construction, transportation, entertainment and so on.

geographical location and availability. Such a service would benefit both the labourers and the potential employers.

This apart, three other pan India initiatives across rural communities and urban slums would help in creating more opportunities to turbocharge the economy. They are: a) Implementation of Engage India, a specialized project that showcases the distinctive competence of rural and urban communities; b) Creation of specialized regional and local planning bodies for rural and urban infrastructure development; and c) The Ten Persons Programme (TPP) whereby ten resource persons are identified per district and used as nodal points to facilitate two way communication with the communities, with a view to identify problem areas as well as implement solutions at the ground level.

All of these can play a vital role in job creation and further help to turbocharge the Indian economy's growth engine.

Engage India: A digital platform should be designed where rural and peri-urban communities can engage with the larger economy as well as with the world at large. Called 'Engage India', this mega digital platform should have space allocated for each of India's 687 districts to be able to put up information on their skills/resources, requirements and the opportunities that they have to offer and/or partnerships that they are looking for with regard to community projects that they would like to initiate.

They could also have data on infrastructure they possess like markets and include useful information such as prevailing prices of commodities and local products available. This would enable greater information exchange between districts, and open up newer markets as well.

From the perspective of foreign investors, this would be a transparent resource enabling them to make rational choices in identifying projects/ communities that they would like to engage with. This platform could even have a corner for investors to share information on proposed projects. The portal could thus democratize and make transparent the process of allocating (economic and other development) projects by allowing the various districts to bid for them through open sharing of information on their suitability, distinctive competencies, the locally available resources and whatever else they have to offer. This would further generate healthy competition between the districts. This would be a true means to achieve the Panchayati Raj[240] style of local governance that is much discussed in India.

Specialized Regional and Local Planning Bodies for Rural and Urban Infrastructure Development: In the context of developing rural and urban infrastructure, it might be useful to set up an independent body on the lines of the National Capital Region Planning Board (NCRPB) at the state and district levels. These bodies should be invested

---

[240] The Panchayati Raj in India generally refers to the system introduced by constitutional amendment in 1992, although it is based upon the traditional panchayat system of South Asia.

with the authority and the responsibility of coordinating all resources and efforts that go into the development of infrastructure within the state and its districts. Such a nodal body is crucial to ensure synergy in planning and execution and to avoid duplication and conflicting goals.

The establishment of planning bodies like NCRPB at the state and district level should also help in combating climate change—through balanced ecologically sustainable growth at the state and district levels. Climate change is a very serious issue, from the perspective of agriculture as well as (indiscriminate) urbanization, both of which suffer from the negative impacts of climate change[241].

Indeed, a key task for these planning bodies would be to coordinate the development and implementation of the nationwide "Smart City" program, another flagship initiative of Prime Minister Narendra Modi's government. Alongside Smart Cities, I also suggest the setting up of "Smart Villages" (in rural areas) and "Smart Townships" (in urban areas), which are completely self sustaining units that are also smart in terms of resource allocation, management and utilisation and governance besides the smartness derived through access to information technology. The key point to note here is that smartness for a city, township and/or village is much more than mere use of information technology. Smartness will not only

---

[241] The examples of Chennai on December 1, 2015 and Mumbai on 26 July, 2005 are cases in point.

depend on the ability of the entity (whether city, township or village) to use its resources and programs smartly across sectors such as electricity, transportation, telecommunications, water, drainage, solid waste management and so on, but also from its ability to reflect its responsiveness and adaptability in its vision, planning, leadership and governance. In other words, smartness will have to come via smart infrastructure, smart decision making and smart leadership.

Further, in such "Smart Villages" and 'Smart Townships", apart from improvements to basic infrastructure (like power, water and sanitation, roads and highways and telecommunications as noted above), it is also crucial to improve employment opportunities by facilitating establishment of industries using local level distinctive competence without compromising on the local rural/urban ecosystem.

It goes without saying that these "Smart Villages" and "Smart Townships" must also provide an improved quality of life, a lifestyle in pursuit of which the rural youth migrate to large urban agglomerations such as metros. Reducing migration into metros, if not reverse migration back to villages and towns is essential—simply because metros and cities are facing tremendous population pressure and their infrastructural capabilities are severely tested.

For example, highway malls with food courts attached and with quality entertainment and recreational facilities may be set up along national highways, to begin with. These could result in significant employment generation and will have the potential to attract huge investment given the as yet untapped potential of rural and semi-urban markets because of the ever burgeoning traffic on highways. But setting up such malls without adequate public transportation may render them a wasteful exercise. In fact, the "smart approach" would be to establish the relevant public transportation infrastructure concurrently, improving the connectivity between villages and such highway centres and also nearby towns/ cities.

If quality public transport is made available at adequate intervals, it would discourage the use of private transport. Besides improving connectivity, it would also relieve the pressure of traffic on roads, apart from cutting down both noise and air pollution levels.

This same "smart approach" needs to be adopted across sectors, whether we are talking about smart cities, smart villages and/or smart townships.

Ten Persons Programme: In a bid to involve citizen's groups in nation building by strengthening local participation in the development process, I propose that a team of ten volunteers is formed at every district to facilitate two way communication between the people and the administration. This will not only help identify the grassroots needs and lacunae in the system but also facilitate the delivery of need based services/projects to the true beneficiaries and without the intervention of exploitative middlemen.

To sum it up, the building blocks need to be strong and aligned correctly for them to endure the ravages of time. Demonetization has highlighted the crevices in these building blocks, something the country has turned a blind eye to for too long now. Hopefully, the opportunity in adversity will be seized and the building blocks will be strengthened for the structure to emerge stronger. If that is done, the pains of demonetization would seem well worth it, even as an era of growth and prosperity for all is ushered in, including those who have been traditionally deprived of the same.

CHAPTER 7

Taming The Corrupt

If there is even a single point of convergence in the demonetization debate, it is the fact that black money is the fuel that keeps the engine of corruption humming. If tax evasion is the seed that brings forth the black money tree, then corruption is the fruit that it bears. The product of an illegal action can neither be acknowledged in the open nor recognized as a component of a lawful transaction. So it needs to be recognized that black money brings forth more corruption, serves to generate more of its kind and the cycle goes on.

What can demonetization truly achieve in the context of corruption? For one, it can extinguish the value of the black money hoarded in the open market. While the declaration on the night of November 8 achieved that, it did give an opportunity for the black money to be brought into the formal financial system at a fraction of its value, with the major portion being absorbed by the state in the form of taxes and penalties. This way, a trail would be established and the tax authorities would keep a closer watch over the sources of the surrendered black money.

The Cinderella Notes

It will take until after December 30 to evaluate how successful the demonetization exercise has been in mopping up the currency in circulation in the form of the SBNs, and the black money component in the same. However, what is distressing is that the exercise does not appear to have completely succeeded in putting the fear of the law in the hearts of all the people.

There have been reports of the corrupt resorting to various techniques including the use of money mules to get their stash of black money white-washed and several bank officials[242] have reportedly been charged with abetting hoarders in having their black money reserves converted to newly minted currency. Hardly a week after the demonetization, two officials[243] of the Kandla port in Gujarat were found to have accepted bribes, in newly minted Rs 2,000 notes. This was not an isolated report, though. There have been too many of them over the last few weeks to dismiss them as such.

Such brazenness, in the face of what can possibly be termed one of the country's biggest and boldest measures against black money, only goes to prove the

[242] See 'Demonetisation: 27 senior bank officials suspended to check corrupt practices', December 2, 2016, *The Times of India*, PTI, http://timesofindia.indiatimes.com/india/Demonetisation-27-senior-bank-officials-suspended-to-check-corrupt-practices/articleshow/55753967.cms
[243] See 'Demonetisation: Three held for accepting bribe in new currency', November 17, 2016, *The Indian Express*, PTI, http://indianexpress.com/article/india/india-news-india/demonetisation-three-held-for-accepting-bribe-in-new-currency-4380715/

point that demonetization can only be the first step, and certainly not the only one, to win the war against black money or corruption. More importantly, this first step has not been a sufficient deterrent for the corrupt that occupy the echelons of power.

So, if we're really serious about eradicating black money, we need to first find ways to uproot the corruption that is at its base. Corruption is, after all, the all-important source of black money and creates a chain of events and practices that become self-sustaining and ultimately, consume the system.

Before we seek ways to put an end to 'corruption', it would be useful to define the term. In my opinion, corruption is a very complex phenomenon, with its roots digging deep into the functioning of political, bureaucratic, commercial and non-governmental institutions and involving a variety of stakeholders in both the public and private sectors.

In definitional terms, corruption is any action (or set of actions) where institutions/people abuse their (public/private) office for private gain. It requires two or more parties acting in concert—parties who are misusing the office and parties who benefit from such misuse. Such an abuse of office for private gain happens when the individuals/institutions concerned accept, solicit, and/or extort a bribe. It is also misuse of power when intermediaries/agents actively offer bribes to circumvent policies and processes for competitive advantage and profit. An act can also be construed as corruption even if no bribery occurs— for example, through patronage and nepotism based on family/other relationships,[244] the theft of state/private institutional assets by people in positions of power,[245] and/or the diversion of state/institutional revenues to private parties.

Corruption can further be categorised as either spectacular corruption (like in the case of various scams—2G Spectrum[246] or Commonwealth Games[247] or Bellary Mines[248] or Coal Block Allocation[249] or Adarsh Housing Society[250] or the Harshad Mehta Scam)[251] or regular corruption (bribes to get things done on a day-to-day basis).

---

[244] See **appendix 5** for examples of the 'revolving door phenomenon' that caused huge conflicts of interest in the United States.

[245] See **appendix 4** for examples of 'conflicts of interests' in the financial sector in the United States.

[246] See 'What is the 2G spectrum scam?', October 19, 2012, *India Today,*
http://indiatoday.intoday.in/story/what-is-the-2g-scam-all-about/1/188832.html

[247] See 'Major scam hits Commonwealth Games', July 31, 2010, *The Hindu,* PTI, http://www.thehindu.com/news/national/Major-scam-hits-Commonwealth-Games/article16215706.ece

[248] See 'Karnataka lost Rs 1 lakh cr from 2006-2010', June 17, 2013, *The Hindu,* Sudipto Mondal,
http://www.thehindu.com/news/national/karnataka/karnataka-lost-rs-1-lakh-cr-from-20062010/article4820758.ece

[249] See 'What's the coal scam about?', March 12, 2015, *The Hindu,* Special Correspondent,
http://www.thehindu.com/news/national/whats-the-coal-scam-about/article6983434.ece

[250] See 'Adarsh scam: The story of a posh high-rise with not-so-posh occupants', April 29, 2016, *The Hindu,* Deepalakshmi K,
http://www.thehindu.com/news/national/Adarsh-scam-The-story-of-a-posh-high-rise-with-not-so-posh-occupants/article14264528.ece

[251] See 'Economic Milestone: Stock Market Scam (1992)', August 20, 2014, *Forbes India Magazine,* Pravin Palande,

The Cinderella Notes

Spectacular corruption is often remembered while the institutionalized day to day corruption in the form of bribery, including corporate bribery, is so entrenched in our system that it is almost accepted as a way of life. However, bribery in general and corporate bribery, in particular, is bad for the environment, especially in a free market economy that India aspires to become—where fair competition should determine who wins at the market place, be it for the supply of products or services rendered. That products and services should compete on the basis of price, quality, service, and other factors is undisputed. Corporate bribery destroys this basic tenet and corporations bribing officials to assist in gaining business is bad practice.

Of course, one must also not forget fraud and associated evils that can and do take place in the private/public sector, often with disastrous and costly results. Many of these result in the accumulation of illegal wealth and black money. Weakly regulated and fraudulent financial systems can undermine people's savings, increase transaction costs, enhance indebtedness and impose high economic costs when they collapse. The 2010 Andhra Pradesh microfinance crisis[252] is a case in point as also the sub-prime crisis[253] in the United States and elsewhere.

---

http://www.forbesindia.com/article/independence-day-special/economic-milestone-stock-market-scam-(1992)/38457/1

[252] See appendix 6 for what happened in the Indian microfinance sector in 2010—called as the 2010 Andhra Pradesh microfinance crisis.

[253] See appendix 4 for what happened in the United States 'sub-prime' mortgages market.

The Satyam Computers fiasco is yet another example worth recalling here. This suggests that corporate crime,[254] which typically takes any of the following forms, is yet another form of corruption that also leads to accumulation of black money. The examples include: a) misrepresentation in financial statements of corporations; b) manipulation in the stock market; c) securities fraud; d) conflicts of interests; e) commercial bribery including that of public officials directly or indirectly; f) embezzlement and misappropriation of funds; g) misapplication of funds in receiverships and bankruptcies; and h) taxation related issues including use of tax havens and so on.

The above, in many ways, suggest the broad context of corruption in India. The key question here is how can this multifaceted phenomenon of corruption be fought so as to eliminate black money emanating from all of these?

One way would be to use the *Lokpal*[255] and its state counterparts (*Lokayuktas*) as an institutional response to fight corruption and thereby possibly curb black money. Indeed, the Indian Parliament passed the

---

[254] See 'The Scam: from Harshad Mehta to Ketan Parekh Also includes JPC FIASCO & Global Trust Bank Scam', *Kensource Information Services Private Limited*, Debshish Basu and Sucheta Dalal, https://www.amazon.in/SCAM-Harshad-Parekh-FIASCO-Global-ebook/dp/B00M8XSXWY, which offers interesting insights regarding securities fraud and related matters.

[255] See 'Why Lokpal eludes India 30 months after Parliament passed a historic law', May 30, 2016, *The Times of India*, Darpan Singh in Mirror Image, http://blogs.timesofindia.indiatimes.com/darpan-singh-blog/why-lokpal-eludes-india-30-months-after-parliament-passed-a-historic-law/

Lokpal and Lokayuktas Act, 2013[256] facilitating the establishment of a Lokpal (Ombudsman) with the specific objective of fighting corruption in public offices and ensuring accountability of all public officials, including the Prime Minister (PM), but with some special safeguards.

As per this law, the *Lokpal* is to consist of a chairperson and a maximum of eight members with 50 percent of them as judicial members and the remaining 50 percent comprising scheduled castes (SC), scheduled tribes (ST), other backward classes (OBCs), minorities and women. The chairperson and members of *Lokpal* are to be selected by a committee consisting of the Prime Minister (PM), the Speaker of the Lok Sabha, the Leader of Opposition in the Lok Sabha and the Chief Justice of India (CJI) or a sitting Supreme Court judge nominated by CJI. An eminent jurist is to be nominated as a fifth member by the President of India on the basis of recommendations of the first four members of the selection committee "through consensus".

Lokpal's jurisdiction is to cover all types and categories of public servants. In addition, all entities (including NGOs) who receive foreign donations— as per the Foreign Contribution Regulation Act (FCRA)—in excess of Rs 10 lakh per year are to come under the purview of the *Lokpal*. Furthermore,

---

[256] See 'The Lokpal And Lokayuktas Act 2013', January 1, 2014, *Ministry Of Law And Justice*, The Gazette Of India Extraordinary Part II, http://www.indiacode.nic.in/acts2014/1%20of%202014.pdf and 'The Lokpal and Lokayuktas Act, 2013', *Wikipedia*, https://en.wikipedia.org/wiki/Lokpal_and_Lokayuktas_Act,_2013

states are to set up their respective *Lokayuktas* through an appropriate state law within 365 days.

The fact of the matter though is that India still does not have a *Lokpal*, even 36 months after the bill was passed in Parliament. Part of the reason for this is the non-availability of the Leader of the Opposition in the Lok Sabha for the search committee.

It is my opinion that the central government must bring an amendment to the *Lokpal* and *Lokayuktas* Act, 2013 that will permit the Leader of the Opposition (in the Rajya Sabha) to be a part of the search committee as there is no recognized Leader of Opposition in the Lok Sabha.

This should facilitate the search committee to function immediately and thereby enable the appointment of the chairperson and members of the *Lokpal* (at the earliest) in a time bound manner. The *Lokpal* must be allotted funds and should become a functioning body at least within six months.

Lokayuktas have been established by only the following states: Andhra Pradesh,[257] Assam,[258]

---

[257] See 'The Andhra Pradesh Lokayukta and Upa Lokayukta (Amendment) Act, 1987', *Laws of India*,
http://www.lawsofindia.org/statelaw/1711/TheAndhraPradeshLoka yuktaandUpaLokayuktaAmendmentAct1987.html
[258] See 'The Assam Lokayukta and Upa-Lokayuktas Act, 1985', *Laws of India*,
http://www.lawsofindia.org/statelaw/6126/TheAssamLokayuktaand UpaLokayuktasAct1985.html

Chattisgarh,[259] Delhi,[260] Gujarat,[261] Haryana,[262] Himachal Pradesh,[263] and Odisha.[264] The central government must engage in dialogue with all other state governments and ensure that they too have functioning *Lokayuktas* in their respective states, at least within a time period of one year.

Here, it must be mentioned that the present government has introduced and passed 'the *Lokpal* and *Lokayuktas* (Amendment[265]) Bill, 2016' in the Lok Sabha[266] to amend the *Lokpal* and *Lokayuktas* Act, 2013 in relation to the declaration of assets and liabilities by public servants[267]. The provisions of the

---

[259] See 'The Chhattisgarh Lok Aayog Act, 2002', *Laws of India*, http://www.lawsofindia.org/statelaw/2851/TheChhattisgarhLokAayogAct2002.html

[260] See 'The Delhi Lokayukta and Upalokayukta Act, 1995', *Laws of India*, http://www.lawsofindia.org/statelaw/2780/TheDelhiLokayuktaandUpalokayuktaAct1995.html

[261] See 'The Gujarat Lokayukta Act, 1986', *Laws of India*, http://www.lawsofindia.org/statelaw/2196/TheGujaratLokayuktaAct1986.html

[262] See 'The Haryana Lokayukta Act, 2002', *Laws of India*, http://www.lawsofindia.org/statelaw/1305/TheHaryanaLokayuktaAct2002.html

[263] See 'The Himachal Pradesh Lokayukta Act, 1983', *Laws of India*, http://www.lawsofindia.org/statelaw/3085/TheHimachalPradeshLokayuktaAct1983.html

[264] See 'The Lokpal and Lokayuktas Act, 1995', *Laws of India*, http://www.lawsofindia.org/statelaw/2626/TheLokpalandLokayuktasAct1995.html

[265] See 'The Lokpal and Lokayuktas (Amendment) Bill, 2016', *PRS India*, http://www.prsindia.org/billtrack/the-lokpal-and-lokayuktas-bill-2016-4354/

[266] On July 27, 2016.

[267] In my opinion, the amendment is likely to weaken the fight against corruption as it is likely to enhance the play of conflict of interest in the public sector.

Bill are to apply retrospectively, from the date of the coming into force of the 2013 Act.

While the *Lokpal* bill has been passed by Parliament, a number of other bills, which will provide a sound basis for tackling corruption, are still pending[268] in Parliament. These include bills related to citizen charter,[269] electronic public service delivery,[270] public procurement[271] and judicial accountability.[272] The *Benami* transactions bill[273] and Whistleblower protection bill[274] have however been passed. Together, all of these bills, when passed, should facilitate the *Lokpal* to deal with the issue of corruption in a more comprehensive manner.

---

[268] At least, as at the time of writing this book.

[269] See 'The Right of Citizens for Time Bound Delivery of Goods and Services and Redressal of their Grievances Bill, 2011 (Citizens Charter)', *PRS India*, http://www.prsindia.org/billtrack/the-right-of-citizens-for-time-bound-delivery-of-goods-and-services-and-redressal-of-their-grievances-bill-2011-2125/, **Current Status: Lapsed**

[270] See 'The Electronic Delivery of Services Bill, 2011', *PRS India*, *http://www.prsindia.org/billtrack/the-electronic-delivery-of-services-bill-2011-2148/*, **Current Status: Lapsed**

[271] See 'The Public Procurement Bill, 2012', *PRS India*, http://www.prsindia.org/billtrack/the-public-procurement-bill-2012-2310/, **Current Status: Lapsed**

[272] See 'The Judicial Standards and Accountability Bill, 2010', *PRS India*, http://www.prsindia.org/billtrack/the-judicial-standards-and-accountability-bill-2010-1399/, **Current Status: Lapsed**

[273] See 'The Benami Transactions (Prohibition) (Amendment) Bill, 2015', *PRS India*, http://www.prsindia.org/billtrack/the-benami-transactions-prohibition-amendment-bill-2015-3789/, **Current Status: Passed**

[274] See 'The Whistle Blowers Protection (Amendment) Bill, 2015', *PRS India*, http://www.prsindia.org/billtrack/the-whistle-blowers-protection-amendment-bill-2015-3784/, **Current Status: Passed by LS**

The Cinderella Notes

While enacting a law is the first step towards curbing corruption, the effectiveness of the law would depend on how well it is implemented on the ground. This leads one to ask, if and when the *Lokpal* arrives, how can the *Lokpal* be made effective to help fight this menace? What are the implications for the design and implementation of the *Lokpal* as an institutionalized response to fight corruption?

First, let us clearly recognise the fact that while the RTI (Right to Information) Act was perhaps the first baby step in this process, an effective *Lokpal* is a big and crucial step.

Second, to be effective, the *Lokpal* must be appropriately designed. Specifically, the scope of the *Lokpal* must clearly be thought out in terms of who the Act will cover and for what kinds of corruption. Care must be devoted to achieving a proper balance keeping in mind practical feasibility and considering the following: (a) A very large (bureaucratic) organisation would become unwieldy and perhaps even counterproductive; and (b) A very narrow scope for the *Lokpal* could reduce effectiveness, especially from the perspective of tackling corruption at the level of the common man. Therefore, deciding on the appropriate scope of *Lokpal* is a very critical issue, if it is to serve as an effective institution on the ground in tackling country wide corruption. It would be prudent to revisit this issue with the chairperson and members of the *Lokpal*, once they are appointed. The same arguments apply to *Lokayuktas* in the various states.

The Cinderella Notes

Third, the *Lokpal* must be truly independent and also be <u>seen</u> to be independent in terms of the process of the selection of its chairperson and members as well as its larger accountability as an institution. The *Lokpal* must, therefore, be established as a fully autonomous body capable of fulfilling the vested mandate. Under no circumstance, should the *Lokpal* be under the tutelage of the people/institutions who are to be investigated (by it). There should be no conflicts of interest whatsoever. The *Lokpal* must also be made accountable to people/institutions who do not fall under its jurisdiction. All of the above would have to apply to the *Lokayuktas* as well. This is a tricky issue and must be addressed—suitably during implementation—if indeed, the *Lokpal* is to be effective in rooting out corruption.

Last, many aspects of corruption (like bribery) call for a giver of the bribe and that calls for significant attitude change across wide sections of society in India. I hope that the *Lokpal,* and the associated *Lokayuktas,* also provide for awareness campaigns that emphasise to the public the need to refrain from giving bribes. This is perhaps the toughest task for the *Lokpal* as without this attitude change among the people, very little can be achieved in fighting corruption. This issue should not be underestimated because, among other things, people would be required to wait for their turn with regard to delivery of products and services and not attempt to jump the queue, when it comes to accessing various goods/services.

The Cinderella Notes

This is certainly a huge task in a country of over a billion people, most of whom are in a tearing hurry and willing to pay to be served out-of-turn. Alternatively, some feel a sense of entitlement by virtue of their position or status and don't think twice before using it to jump the queue. To help fix this issue on the ground, the demand-supply gap in the delivery of goods/services would also have to be reduced and unnecessary bureaucratic approvals/procedures (which are perhaps the cause of this form of bribery in the first place) eliminated. India could also look at the United Kingdom and Bhutan, which have enacted anti-bribery acts that provide disincentives and penal punishments to the bribe-giver. Let us not forget the bribe-giver in this whole matter as without them, much of the corruption would not exist.

Apart from a strong and independent *Lokpal*, a range of other aspects[275] would have to be addressed to eradicate corruption in India. The most important among these are given below:

---

[275] The other aspects are: (1)Political reforms with transparent (state and other) funding of elections which is taken up later in this book; (2) Rationalisation of various taxes to encourage tax payments and facilitate better tax collections, which was addressed earlier in this book; (3) Creation of a citizen's grievance-redressal system that ensures all citizens gain access to all basic services at an appropriate cost when in need of the same; (4) Advocacy and awareness campaigns that ensure citizens commit themselves to not engaging in corrupt practices such as payment of bribes, evasion of taxes, commission of frauds, and the like; and (5) Regulation of critical sectors like financial services, to prevent fraud and corruption in public/private enterprises so as to safeguard people's money (savings), avoid over-indebtedness and the like.

(a) Sound corruption-retarding policies relating to the use of natural resources such as land (and its acquisition), mining, underwater exploration, spectrum, and the like, for a variety of purposes. All of these sectors have been prone to scams, and (b) an appropriate Public Procurement Act relating to the sale/lease of natural (public) resources which have again seen the largest and biggest scams.

India is one of the few countries that does not yet have a law[276] for public procurement and in the context of the various scams that have occurred over the period 1984 to 2013, this cannot go unnoticed[277]. This, in effect, is perhaps the most important measure that the Government of India will now have to take to bring an end to corruption and the generation of black money.

Indeed, public procurement is a very large issue and goes far beyond the proposed website[278] or e-auction process[279] set up by the government. Yet, it has not

---

[276] A Public Procurement Bill[276] was introduced in 2012 in the parliament but it was never enacted.

[277] Although the earlier UPA (United Progressive Alliance) government did introduce the Public Procurement Bill, 2012 in the parliament, it never got enacted—'The Public Procurement Bill, 2012', Bill No. 58 of 2012, As Introduced in *Lok Sabha*, http://164.100.24.219/BillsTexts/LSBillTexts/asintroduced/58_201 2_LS_EN.pdf

[278] An Amazon type of website is said to have been proposed for purchase of items by the government.

[279] 3 G Spectrum was e auctioned. '3G e-auction a first for India on this scale', August 04, 2008, *Livemint*, R. Jai Krishna, http://www.livemint.com/Home-Page/bClR7ymFdhmAy6XG8VO5OJ/3G-eauction-a-first-for-India-on-this-scale.html

been subject to sufficient regulation. The fact that India does not yet have a law for public procurement acquires even greater significance in the face of the multi-faceted scams that occurred during the period 2008 to 2013—many of these concerned public procurement with regard to natural resources such as land, coal, mining and sale of spectrum.

In this context, I would also like to quote from the judgment handed down by Supreme Court Justice Jagdish Singh Kehar[280] in the 2G Spectrum case where he laid down that:

> **"No part of the natural resource can be dissipated as a matter of largesse, charity, donation or endowment, for private exploitation. Each bit of natural resource expended must bring back a reciprocal consideration"[281]**

In his 2015-16 budget speech,[282] the Union Minister Arun Jaitley reiterated his government's commitment to formalising the country's public procurement system as a part of its continuing reforms in public financial management. In a bid to actionize the commitment, the government sought to revamp the bill framed by the previous UPA government. The bill was introduced in the last Lok Sabha by the then

---

[280] Jagdish Singh Kehar is to be the next chief justice of India.

[281] See 'Sans 2G, Presidential Reference maintainable: court', September 28, 2012, The Hindu, J.Venkatesan,
http://www.thehindu.com/news/national/sans-2g-presidential-reference-maintainable-court/article3942879.ece

[282] See 'Revamping public procurement', April 23, 2015, *The Hindu*, Mukul G. AsherTarun Sharma and Shahana Sheikh,
http://www.thehindu.com/opinion/op-ed/revamping-public-procurement/article7130910.ece

Finance Minister Pranab Mukherjee and referred to the Parliamentary Standing Committee on finance in May 2012. Following no report from the Committee, the bill was allowed to lapse with the dissolution of the then Lok Sabha. The present Union Government called for feedback and suggestions on the provisions of the draft bill from civil society, non-government organisations, lawyers and industry bodies.

Some of the provisions proposed by the 2012 Bill are as follows:

- The bill[283] sought to regulate as well as ensure accountability and transparency in (public) procurement by the central government and its various entities. Procurements for disaster management and/or for security/strategic purposes were supposedly exempt from the bill. Likewise, public procurement below Rs 50 lakh was also deemed to be exempted. In addition, the government, at its discretion, was also empowered to exempt, in public interest, any procurement and/or procuring entities from the provisions of the bill.

- The government was empowered to prescribe a code of conduct and integrity for bidder and procuring entity staff and officials. Under certain circumstances, the bill also empowered the government and/or procuring entities to completely debar a bidder, if required.

---

[283]Paraphrased from 'The Public Procurement Bill, 2012', PRS *India,* http://www.prsindia.org/billtrack/the-public-procurement-bill-2012-2310/, **Current Status: Lapsed**

- As per the mandates of the bill, all procurement-related information was to be published in a Central Public Procurement Portal in an open and transparent manner.
- Open Competitive Bidding was the procurement method preferred under the bill; every procuring entity had to provide reasons if it used alternative methods. Conditions and procedures were also specified for use of alternative methods of bidding.
- Procurement Redressal Committees were to be set up as per the mandates of the bill. Such committees could be approached by any aggrieved bidder for suitable remedies and redressal.
- As per the mandates of the bill, both the acceptance of a bribe by a public servant and also the offering of the same by any bidder—with a view to influence the procurement process and outcomes—was punishable with not only a fine but also imprisonment.

Even at the time of the 2012 Bill being tabled in Parliament, there was criticism[284] with regard to its efficacy. A number of problem areas were identified. One was the inexplicable empowerment of the government to exempt certain 'kinds' of procurements from the due public procurement process, and/or even to limit competition and competitive forces in specific cases. Second was the

---

[284] See 'The Public Procurement Bill, 2012', *PRS India,*
http://www.prsindia.org/billtrack/the-public-procurement-bill-2012-2310/, **Current Status: Lapsed**

apparent reference to Open Competitive Bidding as the preferred method of procurement, even without defining the term precisely. The third was the absence of a requirement of appropriate certification by a competent technical authority (or expert) in the event of the need to source from a specific supplier, with the objective of ensuring standardization and/or enabling compatibility with existing systems. The non-restriction of the use of cost-plus contracts, which provide lesser incentive for efficiency was the fourth.

While recognizing these limitations, I would like to state that the following fundamental issues[285] should be considered while redrafting/recasting the framework proposed by the previously tabled 2012 legislation.

The first deals with transparency in public procurement. The law must ensure that there is an adequate degree of transparency in the whole (public) procurement cycle so as to facilitate fair and equitable treatment for all potential suppliers. Transparency must be maximised in competitive tendering and precautionary measures must be in place to enhance integrity, for (any) exceptions made to competitive tendering (in case of urgency and/or national security).

---

[285] This chapter draws on several resources including information from various civil society organisations, multi-lateral and bi-lateral agencies, international organisations like the Organisation for Economic Co-operation and Development (OECD) and other stakeholders. They are gratefully acknowledged.

The Cinderella Notes

Among other things, the law would also have to ensure the following aspects.

1. All potential suppliers/contractors must have clear and consistent information with regard to the whole procurement process and understand it well.
2. Where required, the degree of transparency may be adapted according to the recipient of information and the stage of the cycle. In other words, confidential information (trade secrets) would need to be protected to ensure a level playing field for potential suppliers, and also prevent possible collusion among stakeholders.
3. The public procurement process should be applied equitably/fairly across the entire cycle by all stakeholders and should be perceived to be fair and equitable.
4. The drive for transparency should not create unnecessary 'red tape' and inefficiency in the public procurement system, thereby causing unnecessary and huge delays.
5. Key decisions made on public procurement should be well-documented and easily accessible for examination by various stakeholders, as appropriate.
6. Relevant stakeholders (including auditors) should be able to check and determine whether specifications are unbiased and/or award decisions based on fair grounds.
7. Clear rules and concrete guidance must exist with regard to the choice of the procurement method and on exceptions to competitive tendering (if any).

The Cinderella Notes

All of this suggests that, for good procurement regulations, systems must not be unnecessarily complex, costly and/or time-consuming. These could cause huge delays (in the procurement) and discourage participation, especially by micro, small and medium enterprises (MSMEs).

In fact, excessive red tape in such public procurement regulations may create significant opportunities for (fresh) corruption. This would surely result in the whole purpose of enacting the legislation becoming counter-productive.

Therefore, ensuring an adequate level of transparency that enhances corruption control, while not impeding the efficiency and the effectiveness of the public procurement process, is a challenge that needs to be met by using the mantra of 'balanced enabling regulation'. I hope that the government keeps these aspects in mind while drafting the much-needed Public Procurement Act in India.

Second, the decision making process, with regard to public procurement, should be transparent in the sense of being well documented and accessible. The criteria should be clear, objective, reliable and valid, in the sense that anyone applying the said criteria will be able to come to the same (similar) judgment. This takes us to the next aspect of public procurement.

With a transparent decision making process and objective, reliable and valid criteria, it should be easy for the CAG[286] and team to revalidate the same, if required subsequently. It goes without saying that trade secrets (if any) of the participant stakeholders should be protected to prevent misuse by others.

Other aspects that such an Act should focus on include:

- Conflict of interest management of public sector officials including risks and vulnerability;
- Protection of whistleblowers;
- Internal controls to ensure that the implementation progresses as intended;
- Cycle of audits for the procurement to ensure that the funds are utilized as originally proposed and intended and also to check for action taken reports on previous audits;
- Appropriate grievance redressal mechanisms for the suppliers and other stakeholders; and
- Empowerment of civil society organisations, media and the wider public to scrutinise public procurement.

I fervently hope that these factors will be kept in mind and a freshly drafted Public Procurement Bill will be tabled in Parliament at the earliest opportunity and subsequently enacted as law.

If efforts are not made to weed out corruption, which is the fount of black money, the demonetization exercise would prove to be a case of addressing a superficial symptom even while leaving

---

[286] The Comptroller and Auditor General (CAG) of India.

the root cause untouched. Appointment of *Lokpal/Lokayuthas* and enacting legislation on public procurement are crucial weapons that the government needs in its armoury if it is to really win the war on corruption that it is currently waging. To be prepared is half the victory after all!

CHAPTER 8

Dirty Money

In the earlier chapter on corruption, I had attempted to classify corruption into two kinds—regular corruption and spectacular corruption. The first kind, regular corruption, is what we experience almost on a day to day basis—the little *baksheesh*[287] that is paid to get a certificate from a public authority, to get a file 'passed', to get the traffic cop to overlook a jumped signal or to gain access to a facility/service out of turn. This kind of corruption has been institutionalized to the point where we have ceased to consider it 'bribes' or 'corrupt acts'.

The second kind most often falls in the realm of political corruption. The headline hogging scams which cost the exchequer millions and millions of rupees, more often than not, involve those in political office. This corruption at 'the highest levels' is, after all, possible only with the tacit, if not overt, involvement of those occupying the highest echelons of power.

---

[287] https://www.merriam-webster.com/dictionary/baksheesh — "Baksheesh" is from Persian "bakhshīsh," which is also the source of the word *buckshee,* meaning "something extra obtained free," "extra rations," or "windfall, gratuity."

Political corruption is defined as the use of power by public officials for their illegitimate, private gain. While public officials include those elected/appointed to office, we will be restricting our discussion to political parties/elected peoples' representatives for the purpose of this chapter.

There are different kinds of political corruption, all of which yield personal/political gain to the elected officials. Misuse of power and office might happen for pecuniary benefit or to subvert the democratic or electoral process to win elections.

In the context of misusing power for pecuniary benefits, the beneficiaries of the political largesse are most often industrial or corporate houses. They use political donations as a tool to further short-term business interests or to establish ties[288] with political parties with an eye to long-term benefits. There are also specific instances where corporates bid for rights/licenses to commercially exploit public resources, or submit tenders to meet the procurement needs of the government. In a bid to influence the public officials to award such contracts/licenses to them, commissions/cuts are offered on the total value of the said contracts to politicians in positions of power. The bribes may also take the form of land, gold, stock or other assets.

---

[288] This can happen through lobbying, for instance. The 'Nira Radia tapes controversy' is a case in point—see
https://en.wikipedia.org/wiki/Radia_tapes_controversy

The Cinderella Notes

Where political donations are used as a means to lobby for legislation/public policies, the intent is to further long-term business interests. Generous donations are made to the war chests of the political parties, to finance their various electoral battles. This type of corruption could well be described as institutional corruption, since the benefit accrues to the institution or the political party in this context. Corporates/Business Houses/Individuals bankroll the election campaigns of those political parties, whose rise to power would benefit their interests. There are often instances of the same corporate house funding political parties with opposing ideologies or agendas. This is hardly surprising since the relationship with the political party is established purely to gain access to power circles rather than any significant ideological allegiance. Making payouts to multiple political parties is also a means of hedging their bets.

Some of the money that goes to line political coffers may well be legitimate, clean money. That is, the money has come through a formal financial channel, has been accounted for, and on which taxes have been paid. Some of it may take the informal route, either in the form of 'black money' hoarded within the country in the form of cash stashed away in offshore accounts. The offshore 'money' may go into the offshore accounts of persons connected with the political parties, to be routed back to India through various means, some of which may not even be legal[289]. While this would make political parties complicit in money laundering activities, the monies received thus might not be reflected in the declarations or financial statements of the political parties. In that case, they would be used to fund the 'not so above board' electoral activities like the rigging of polls by the use of muscle power, or by bribing the voters in cash or kind[290] or any other 'off-the-record' activity.

Any money paid to a political party with the intent of gaining a toehold in the corridors of power could be construed as 'dirty money', since the money is a pay-out for future benefits. Through lobbying and offering pecuniary benefits to influence the process of awarding government contracts and licenses, it goes without saying that corporate interests are gaining at the cost of public interest. It is befitting to brand the money that helps business or corporate interests triumph over public interests as 'tainted' or 'dirty' in intent.

Making political donations is not an illegal act or a crime. Such donations can and indeed often do take the form of 'clean' money routed through banking channels. Even if they do not constitute a quid pro quo in the present, like in the case of payouts for contracts/licenses etc, they do represent a promise

---

[289] Most often, they come through what is called as the *'Hawala'* route—See https://en.wikipedia.org/wiki/Hawala

[290] See "Cash for votes a way of political life in South India', March 16, 2011, *The Hindu,* Sarah Hiddleston, http://www.thehindu.com/news/the-india-cables/lsquoCash-for-votes-a-way-of-political-life-in-South-Indiarsquo/article14949621.ece

for the future. The institution/political party is under an implicit obligation to serve the interests/agenda of the corporate/business house making the donation. Where large businesses and/or people with vested interests contribute to any campaign, they are bound to extract their pound of flesh eventually, if not upfront, effectively setting up a conflict of 'interests'.

Unlike the United States of America or the United Kingdom, both of which essentially have a two party system, India is a land of several political parties, espousing a mix of ideologies and sporting a range of colors. According to Section 29B of the Representation of People's Act[291] (RPA), 1951, each and every political party is permitted to accept voluntary contributions given to it by any person or company, other than a Government company or any local body wholly or partly financed by the Government.

Section 182 of Companies Act[292], 2013 states two major conditions with regard to companies desirous of making contributions to political parties: 1) they must have been in existence for a minimum period of three years; and 2) they can donate, at most, 7.5 percent of their profit in a year and they are mandated to clearly identify and appropriately

---

[291] See 'The Representation Of The People Act, 1951', Act No.43 of 1951, July 17, 1951,
http://lawmin.nic.in/legislative/election/volume%201/representatio n%20of%20the%20people%20act,%201951.pdf
[292] See 'The Companies Act, 2013', (No . 18 Of 2013), August 29, 2013, *Ministry Of Law And Justice*, The Gazette of India,
http://www.mca.gov.in/Ministry/pdf/CompaniesAct2013.pdf

disclose the amount donated in their profit and loss account.

Furthermore, no electoral candidate, political party and/or office-bearer thereof can accept any contribution from a source defined as "foreign" under Section 2 of the Foreign Contribution (Regulation) Act[293], 1976. However, an amendment to the above was made in the form of the Foreign Contribution (Regulation) Act, 2010[294] and this redefined the term "foreign source". As per the original provision, a foreign source included any company with foreign investment greater than 50 percent in the Indian entity, while the amendment stated that as long as a foreign company's ownership in an Indian entity was within the (foreign investment) limits prescribed by the Government of India for that specific sector/industry, the company will be treated as "Indian" for the purposes of the FCRA.

Also, as per Section 29 C of the RPA, all registered political parties in India are mandated to submit to the Election Commission (EC) details of all donations received in excess of Rs 20,000 from any person and/or a company. This is in addition to the

---

[293] See 'Foreign Contribution (Regulation) Act, 1976', Act No. 49 of Year 1976,
http://jhpolice.gov.in/sites/default/files/ForeignContributionRegul ationAct_1976.pdf
[294] See 'The Foreign Contribution (Regulation) Act, 2010', No.42 Of 2010, September 26, 2010, *Ministry Of Law And Justice*, The Gazette of India,http://lawmin.nic.in/ld/regionallanguages/THE%20FOREIG N%20CONTRIBUTION%20(REGULATION)%20ACT,2010.%20 (42%20OF%202010).pdf

regular annual tax returns that they are required to file with the tax authorities. Here, it needs to be noted that as per Section 13A[295] of the Income Tax (I-T) Act, political parties do not have to pay any income tax on contributions received. This is however subject to certain specific conditions such as having the accounts audited, disclosing all details about donations received beyond the permissible limit and so on.

While Section 29C of the RPA 1951, prescribes a disclosure limit, political parties have typically been known to work their way around it. The limit laid down by the Act is to be applied to the aggregate of the various sums donated to a political party by an individual or entity or a company in a given year. The political parties have however interpreted the limit to be applicable to donations made in excess of twenty thousand rupees at one time. There are reported instances of donations being broken down into multiple contributions—each just under the permissible limit of Rs 20,000 and the donor being issued multiple receipts. It must be mentioned here that all such restrictions are applicable only to 'official' contributions made through formal banking channels.

Donations by way of cash are practically outside the purview of the Act and remain unknown and undisclosed unless the political party itself chooses to make it public. To the best of my knowledge, as on

---

[295] See 'Tax Exemption to Political Parties [Section 13A]—Income Tax', *TaxDose.com*, http://www.taxdose.com/tax-exemption-to-political-parties-section-13a-income-tax/

date, there is no law that prohibits contributions to political parties in the form of cash. The only issue here is that such contributions are not eligible to be claimed as tax deductions[296] by the donors while computing their net taxable incomes. In fact, according to the Association of Democratic Reforms[297] (ADR), the income tax returns filed by the political parties—which were obtained using the Right to Information Act (RTI)—revealed that a meagre 20 percent of the income of political parties came from contributions disclosed by them to the EC as per Section 29C. This, in effect, means that, the source is neither clearly identifiable nor established for as much as three-quarters of their income—a fact that hints at the significant cash (possibly 'black money') component in the contributions received. The ADR analysis of the total income and expenditure incurred by national parties during FY 2014-15, as declared by these parties in their IT Returns submitted to the ECI, further highlights several other anomalies including incomplete details of donors, duplicate PAN details and cheque numbers and so on.

---

[296] Under Sections 80-GGB and 80-GGC of the Income Tax Act, 1961, political donations made by companies and individuals are permissible as deductions while computing the net taxable income, so long as such contributions are made by way of cheque. The political party to which a donation is being made must be registered under Section 29A of the Representation of the People Act, 1951.
[297] See 'The Foreign Hand In Political Funding', October 17, 2016, *Association for Democratic Reforms (ADR)*, Indian Legal, http://adrindia.org/content/foreign-hand-political-funding

The Cinderella Notes

The National Commission to Review the Working of the Constitution[298], 2001 noted that the dire necessity for taking funds for fighting elections is the base foundation on which the whole architecture of corruption[299] rests. It has been further argued that this is a vicious cycle where the proceeds of corruption are used to fund election campaigns and the victorious campaigns, in turn, lead to more (political) corruption by subverting principles of justice, fairness and equity.

The other aspect of political corruption is that it involves the rigging of elections and subversion of the democratic process—both of which again come at a huge price. Increasingly, there is this reported trend in India of political parties bribing[300] voters in cash or kind, which in effect translates into 'buying' their way into power. According to Election Commission estimates, more than Rs.3,500 Crores (approximately $750 million) was reportedly paid as a bribe[301] during the assembly elections in five Indian states during April-May 2011.

---

[298] The National Commission to Review the Working of the Constitution was set up vide Government Resolution dated 22 February, 2000, http://lawmin.nic.in/ncrwc/ncrwcreport.htm

[299] See 'A Consultation Paper On Review Of Election Law, Processes And Reform Options' NCRW- Final Report Book 1
http://lawmin.nic.in/ncrwc/finalreport/v2b1-9.htm

[300] See "Cash for votes a way of political life in South India', March 16, 2011, *The Hindu,* Sarah Hiddleston,
http://www.thehindu.com/news/the-india-cables/lsquoCash-for-votes-a-way-of-political-life-in-South-Indiarsquo/article14949621.ece

[301] See 'Delayed electoral reforms', January 18, 2012, *The New Indian Express,* Aditya Swarup,
http://www.newindianexpress.com/opinions/2012/jan/18/delayed-electoral-reforms-331363.html

The Cinderella Notes

It is thus clearly established that there is an inextricable link between political funding, corruption and black money generation. Unless we strike at the root of corruption, the black money tree is not going to be felled. Without addressing the institutional (political) corruption that forms the base on which the superstructure is erected, corruption is not going to be uprooted. Sam van der Staak, Programme Manager, International IDEA (an inter-governmental organization that supports sustainable democracy), has identified numerous legal anomalies in India in the context of political funding[302]. These include: a) The lack of a comprehensive election campaign finance act; b) Neither candidates nor political parties have donation or spending limits; c) Anonymous donations are banned in respect of political parties, but not candidates; d) Neither political parties nor candidates have stringent (fool proof) reporting requirements; e) State funding of elections does not exist,; and f) There are no formal penalties for funding violations.

At this juncture, it would be appropriate to recall the Supreme Court notice[303] to the Election Commission and the Central Government on the petition to get political parties under the Right to Information Act

---

[302] See 'The Foreign Hand In Political Funding', October 17, 2016, *Association for Democratic Reforms (ADR)*, Indian Legal, http://adrindia.org/content/foreign-hand-political-funding
[303] See 'Parties under RTI: SC sends notice to Election Commission, Centre', July 8, 2015, *The Indian Express,* Express News Service, http://indianexpress.com/article/india/politics/supreme-court-notice-to-centre-on-plea-to-get-political-parties-under-rti/

(RTI). The government in response[304] indicated that political parties will not be able to divulge details about their institutional functioning and financial matters under the Right to Information (RTI) Act as it would "hamper their smooth functioning" and make them vulnerable to "rivals with malicious intentions". It also pointed out that transparency on financial aspects has already been mandated and enforced under the IT Act, 1961 and the RPA, 1951.

The Election Commission (EC) has also reportedly asked the government to make graft[305] a cognizable offence during elections and has further sought to be empowered to countermand polls in the event of large scale bribery of voters. In this context, it must be recalled that in the May 2016 elections[306] to the Tamil Nadu State Assembly, the EC took the strong, bold and decisive step of countermanding the polls in two assembly constituencies following reports of large scale bribing of the electorate.

The Commission is also reportedly planning a comprehensive review of the sixty- five year old

---

[304] See 'Can't bring political parties under RTI, Centre tells Supreme Court', August 24, 2015, *The Hindu*, Krishnadas Rajagopal, http://www.thehindu.com/news/national/political-parties-cant-be-under-rti-act-centre-tells-sc/article7575584.ece

[305] See 'Make bribing voters a cognizable offence: Election Commission tells govt', December 4, 2016 *The Times of India*, Bharti Jain, http://timesofindia.indiatimes.com/india/Make-bribing-voters-a-cognizable-offence-Election-Commission-tells-govt/articleshow/55782208.cms

[306] See 'A first: Tamil Nadu poll cancelled over bribing voters', May 29, 2016, *The Indian Express*, Express News Service, http://indianexpress.com/article/india/india-news-india/tamil-nadu-election-commission-cancels-polls-to-two-assembly-seats-2823249/

Representation of the People Act to evaluate its ability to deal with the present day challenges and suggest suitable revisions in the form of a draft Bill. In this context, it is reported that they are considering adapting the best practices of foreign governments. For example, the Canadian law mandates that voter education be incorporated in the curriculum of educational institutions—the EC is said to be considering making a similar provision in the revised RPA.

One of the reforms undertaken in recent times with regard to corporate donations to political parties has been the enactment of the **'Electoral Trusts Scheme, 2013'**[307] in order to streamline the process of campaign finance and also ensure the transparency with regard to corporate funding of political parties' and election expenses.

According to this scheme, Electoral Trust companies are promised tax benefits in proportion to the funds they provide to various political outfits. These companies are required to have the term 'Electoral Trust' prefixed to their names and, thereafter, be accredited under the Electoral Trusts Scheme, 2013, in order to differentiate them from companies incorporated under **Section 25 of the Companies Act, 1956.**

The companies are allowed tax benefits only if they satisfy the condition that they distribute 95 percent

---

[307]See 'Functions of electoral trusts',
http://www.incometaxindia.gov.in/Rules/Income-
Tax%20Rules/2008/103120000000009096.htm

of total contributions received by them (in any financial year) to registered political parties within the same year itself. Furthermore, the Electoral Trust companies are not allowed to accept contributions from foreign citizens and/or overseas companies. They are also required to take the PAN number of all contributors who are resident Indians and the passport number of NRI citizens at the time of receiving the contributions.

The Electoral Trusts can possibly be compared to the Super PACs (although not in terms of incorporation) that facilitate indirect campaign finance contributions[308] by corporations to the funds of United States politicians running for office. However, Super PACs are established for specific candidates and there are restrictions on how the funds collected can be deployed. It must be mentioned here that there is a strong movement within the United States people to abolish[309] the Super PACs system.

As can be seen from the above, without a doubt, the present campaign finance system in India appears to be actively fostering an environment where conflicts of interests and corruption thrive. While *'dirty money'* and a corrupt campaign finance system impede the ability to promote freedom and democracy, fight poverty, and tackle corruption, crime and terrorism,

---

[308] In the United States, direct corporate donations to individual political campaigns are forbidden.
[309] See 'CfA Files Federal Lawsuit Against the FEC to Abolish Super PACs', November 4, 2016, *Campaign for Accountability*, http://campaignforaccountability.org/cfa-files-federal-lawsuit-against-the-fec-to-abolish-super-pacs/

more importantly, they prevent the establishment of a *'government by the people, for the people and of the people'*[310]*.'*

The need of the hour is a comprehensive review of existing electoral legislations. They should be revised where necessary to ensure regulation and transparency of donations made to political parties/ politicians. There is also the need to make political parties accountable to the voting public, in terms of their funding sources and the purposes for which the funds are deployed.

In this regard, I would like to make the following suggestions to the EC as it contemplates comprehensive revisions to the existing The Representation of the People Act. It would be beneficial to study and adopt best practices followed in democracies the world over in this context.

Limits on spending: Realistically limit the extent of spending by a candidate for the office of President of India, Vice-President of India, Member of Parliament (Lok Sabha), Member of Parliament (Rajya Sabha), Member of Legislative Assembly (MLA), Member of Legislative Council (MLC) and the various candidates in local body elections. This needs to be done every five years.

---

[310] See 'The Gettysburg Address', Nicolay Copy, Gettysburg, Pennsylvania, November 19, 1863,
http://www.abrahamlincolnonline.org/lincoln/speeches/gettysburg.htm

Regulate funding sources: While corporate funding of elections is widely prevalent in the United States and countries of the European Union (the United Kingdom and Germany, for instance), the history and practice of corporate funding in these countries warns us of the pitfalls of excessive reliance on such donations. France leads by example in this context, having banned all political contributions from legal entities—including corporations. They place the principle of equality of candidates ahead of personal liberty in this context, not wanting to give an advantage to political parties/politicians simply by virtue of having access to larger electoral war chests. Failure to comply with both the substantive and procedural rules of election campaign financing can attract fines as well as render candidates ineligible for public office.

I would suggest an emulation of the French model in this context, imposing a blanket ban on corporations and companies contributing to campaign finances in India, and also imposing penalties including being rendered ineligible to contest in the event of flagrant violation of the rules.

Today, much[311] of the campaign finance comes from powerful corporate interests and it must be emphasized that there is no free lunch. For example, the finance, real estate, insurance and several other industries—that have a keen interest in legislation—

---

[311] See 'Who funds political parties? 90 percent of donations in 2013-2014 came from corporates', December 25, 2014, *First Post*, FP Staff, http://www.firstpost.com/politics/funds-political-parties-90-percent-donations-2013-2014-came-corporates-2015067.html

have contributed significantly in the past. Candidates for office feel obliged to tap into the currency chests of these special interests in order to get their messages out and run competitive campaigns.

Although there is a cap on corporate donations as prescribed by the Companies Act, 2013, laws are circumvented by making contributions in cash and other forms (often constituting the black money component of campaign donations) that fly under the EC's radar.

The only major alternative is to self-fund, which many people cannot afford. An electoral system that relies on candidates to be either super-wealthy or pander to powerful special interests in order to fundraise is effectively broken. A better system would be to publicly finance viable candidates. This would permit candidates who have received a qualifying number of small contributions to receive public financing for their campaigns, making them accountable only to the general public and not to special interests.

Senior journalist M.K.Venu, in a published article, even makes a case[312] for "the Centre to consider levying a cess or tax for the purpose of funding political parties and the elections." He argues that even if a minuscule tax of 0.5 percent of GDP is collected over five years from corporates and high net worth individual tax payers, a corpus of about Rs.

---

[312] See 'Time to Institutionalise Funding of Political Parties', April 17, 2016, *The Wire*, M.K. Venu, http://thewire.in/29984/time-to-institutionalise-funding-of-political-parties/

60,000 crores will become available, for the Election Commission to administer as a constitutional body. His rationale is that, if such funds are put in a common pool controlled and regulated by the EC, the probability of direct deal—making between big companies and political parties stands minimizsed. Under such circumstances, the Election Commission can itself monitor the acquisition of airtime on national broadcast channels, to enable the political parties to make their 'pitch' to the voting population. This would completely obviate the need for huge expenditure on various broadcast and outdoor media to drive home their 'political messages'.

Limits on individual contributions: Given the ban on corporate financing of elections, at the present time, I would propose capping the election contribution of any individual to any political party and/or candidate at Rs 100,000 during a year, with all money being routed through the bank. I would propose curbing the total election related donations from an individual at Rs 500,000 per year. These limits can be suitably revised every five years to make adjustments to the time value of money. In addition, it is suggested that all contributions to political parties, irrespective of the amount donated, must be accompanied by a unique personal identity—be it passport, Aadhar Card, voter ID or PAN card. This would be part of 'know your contributor' (KYC) norms for political parties just as financial institutions have 'know your customer' (KYC) requirements for their clients.

The Cinderella Notes

Action against voter bribery: Make bribery a cognizable offense before, during and after an electoral campaign with suitable deterrents for the voting public too. The voting public especially need to be made to understand that they are 'selling' themselves cheap, since the election eve bribes make politicians feel entitled to the 'powers and privileges' that they have 'paid' for as well as eliminate any sense of accountability to the voting public until the dawn of the next electoral cycle.

Perks and benefits: Bar candidates from accepting perks and privileges, like the use of corporate jets for example, during the campaign process.

Eliminate cash donations: Mandate that all contributions to individual candidates and political parties occurs through banking channels. Stipulate that contributions to individual candidates and political parties to be made digitally.

Maintenance of public database: Facilitate the creation and maintenance of a database, which is a compendium of all the above information (on the lines of the database maintained by the Federal Election Commission (FEC) in the United States in its site www.fec.gov), within one month of the monies having been received by the candidates. There will have to be regular filings once a person has announced his/her candidature. This would ensure transparency as envisaged by the RPA and impose a sense of accountability even without political parties falling under the ambit of the RTI.

The Cinderella Notes

The American model is worthy of emulation here, also because there are strict public disclosure legislations for both federal candidates and Political Action Committees (PACs). Donations by corporations[313] to political parties are disclosed by respective political parties and disseminated by the media to ensure greater public awareness.

To sum it up, political (institutional) corruption is established to be the base on which the entire super structure of illegal money, nepotism, vested interests and exploitation rests. If the professed goal of demonetization, the culling of black money from the economy, is to be achieved, it is imperative to strike at the roots. Unless the base of political corruption is shaken, the edifice of black money will not crumble. A mere crack or two can be plastered over in no time. Rather than chipping away at the cracks to get them to widen, it would benefit the economy to detonate the base and bring the structure down in its entirety. It is hoped that the political parties will treat the rot within the system rather than restricting their focus to the symptoms alone.

---

[313] As noted earlier, I recommended that India follow the French model of banning corporate financing of elections.

CHAPTER 9

The Beginning

It might seem a bit of paradox that the last chapter of the book is titled *'The Beginning'*. Or maybe not; considering demonetization has been like a system reboot in many ways for the economy and the need now is to focus on the road ahead. What does it hold for India—will this beginning mark a truly fresh start or will it simply be more of the same?

The stated objectives of the demonetization exercise were the flushing out of the unaccounted and/or black money and counterfeit notes from the economy. While it can be described as a war on terrorism in the context of the latter, the former is a bit more complex. This is because the Indian economy has been predominantly cash driven, with an entire parallel economy in place.

Even though the incomes of a good majority of people subsisting in the parallel economy fall within the tax exemption limit prescribed by the authorities, the money still falls into the unaccounted category. This is because the monies from this parallel economy are not routed through the formal banking channels.

The Cinderella Notes

At this juncture, it is important to make a crucial distinction between black money, which traditionally has the connotation of being a byproduct of illegal or unlawful transactions, and the unaccounted money of the small producers, artisans, service providers, MSMEs etc. in the parallel economy. Black money is thus only a part of, and not all of, the currency that is circulated through the parallel economy.

It goes without saying that integration of the parallel economy with the formal economy would generally be a positive consequence, since it would make available increased resources for growth and development initiatives. All other issues notwithstanding, it must be admitted that but for demonetization, the money from the parallel economy would have continued to remain out of the formal banking system for a much longer time. Multiple strategies adopted to achieve absorption of the cash circulating in the parallel economy into the banking system have failed, owing to a variety of reasons. Demonetization, in 2016, has largely achieved this objective. No pain, no gain is an oft quoted maxim. However, it must be said that pain could have been mitigated and its management better achieved in the context of demonetization.

Going back to the primary objectives of the mission, it can be safely assumed that most (if not all) black money reserves—in the form of the notified currency—seem to be finding their way into bank accounts, either through that of the holder or a third party. Some of it could possibly have been converted into gold and/or real estate. There were media reports[314] that some black money reserves had been discarded and/or destroyed.

As discussed in the earlier chapters, mechanisms are already in place to assess the pattern of deposits made into banks/post office accounts during the demonetization window and the government is now faced with the challenging task of separating the wheat from the chaff. They need to identify the black money component from among the deposits of the SBNs and take necessary action as required against hoarders, if any. It is also incumbent on the government to continue the war on black money by attacking the reserves maintained in other forms. They need to trace the black money stored as gold and/or real estate. That genuine people must not be troubled by this measure is an aspect that goes without saying.

There is also the urgent need to bring back black money stashed away as cash in offshore banks accounts in tax havens or as real estate acquisitions in foreign lands. Domestic legislation, as well as agreements with foreign governments, are already in place for the government to follow through on this. One hopes that, in the days to come, efforts in those directions will also yield fruit.

---

[314] The interested reader may want to refer to media reports, in the days after the demonetization—see for example, 'One week after demonetisation announcement, crores of old currency notes burned, destroyed, dumped', November 16, 2016, *BS Web Team*, Business Standard, http://www.business-standard.com/article/current-affairs/demonetisation-effect-one-week-after-announcement-crores-old-currency-notes-burned-destroyed-dumped-116111600335_1.html

The Cinderella Notes

On the issue of purging counterfeit notes from the economy, the other objective of demonetization, the exercise has, hopefully, succeeded in disarming the terror/insurgency outfits, the bulk of whose activities are fuelled by fake currency. Although there have been reports of fake notes of the newly minted currency being recovered, the DEA[315] Secretary Shaktikanta Das has assured the country that the possibility of counterfeiting the new notes[316] is very low.

Among the questions that now lie before us is how permanent the effect of demonetization is going to be. For example, while it has certainly succeeded in routing the currency floating in the parallel economy into the formal banking system, the question remains as to whether this will be a one-off effect or if it will result in a more permanent attitudinal and behavioral change in the economy.

The truth is that those excluded from the financial system, whether by choice or by the lack of access, have now been arm twisted into joining the mainstream to protect the value of their cash reserves in demonetized currency. In the days to come, will the formal system be able to retain its hold on this fresh clientele, providing them with better and

---

[315] DEA stands for The Department of Economic Affairs, Ministry of Finance, Government of India.
[316] See 'New notes can't be counterfeited, says DEA Secretary Shaktikanta Das', December 16, 2016, *The Financial Express*, http://www.financialexpress.com/india-news/new-notes-cant-be-counterfeited-says-dea-shaktikanta-das/475364/

simpler access and also making it worth their while to remain included?

While much depends on how the formal financial systems, whether it is the banks or the digital financial service providers, respond to the opportunity ahead of them, it is certainly no easy task to break the centuries-old obsession with cash, which is still the most flexible and convenient method of making transactions, at least from a low-income person's perspective.

On the flip side, though, the fallout of demonetization has left a lasting impact on the common man's psyche, pretty much ensuring that he is never going to feel the same about cash. This is not surprising because what he thought of as his most liquid asset ceased to be fungible in the open market overnight, leaving him with no option but to deposit/exchange it within the formal financial system. Memories of the hardships associated with the process won't go away in a hurry, so deep is the impact.

While there is still time before we can truly pronounce judgment on the success of the demonetization mission given the long-term objectives, the short-term consequences in terms of the impact on the various economic activities and also on overall growth, have been documented sufficiently in the media. I have also tried to address the same in Chapter 2 of this book.

The Cinderella Notes

Though a cost-benefit or a SWOT analysis normally precedes any initiative with a potential for far-reaching consequences, we are, of course, not privy to whether such an exercise was carried out by the establishment. However, in hindsight and in the wake of the huge implementation related issues, one is forced to wonder about the degree of preparedness of our economic system to absorb such a seismic shift.

Efficiency levels have come under question as also the ability to anticipate and second guess the moves of those forces that are opposed to any move to cleanse the economy of corruption. Corruption is so deep-rooted and so deeply entrenched within the institutional hierarchy that some of those entrusted with the task of cleansing the system have themselves colluded with the 'corrupt forces'. It has been disconcerting to read of the complicity[317] of officials even within the central banking authority, not to mention the banking officials[318], in enabling 'corrupt forces' to get their demonetized notes exchanged or to gain access to freshly minted notes, overriding the legitimate needs of the larger population.

---

[317] See 'Demonetisation: RBI official, JDS leader in CBI net', December 13, 2016, *The Economic Times*, PTI, http://economictimes.indiatimes.com/news/politics-and-nation/senior-rbi-official-arrested-for-illegal-currency-exchange/articleshow/55957443.cms

[318] See 'Demonetisation: 27 public sector bank officials suspended over corrupt practices, 6 transferred', December 2, 2016, *First Post*, PTI, http://www.firstpost.com/india/demonetisation-27-public-sector-bank-officials-suspended-over-corrupt-practices-6-transferred-3136880.html

The Cinderella Notes

A critical learning from the demonetization process has been the need to strengthen the system's preparedness in dealing with macro-level changes at short notice and the meticulous planning that perforce needs to precede the same. While some glitches are excusable given the mammoth size of the task, it has to be said that there were some glaring planning errors that ought to have been avoided. For example, the resizing of the newly minted two thousand rupee note is inexplicable, given the resultant need for recalibration of thousands of ATMs, a task that further delayed the process of issuing fresh currency to replace the SBNs.

Second, the issuance of 2000 rupee notes alone as a replacement for the SBNs in the immediate aftermath of demonetization further queered the pitch, with a lot of people refusing to accept the note as they did not have sufficient change to offer in return, especially when the purchases were for less than five hundred rupees. A more judicious mix of denominations could have been adopted and this might have reduced the hardship brought about by 'lack of change'.

Third, as pointed out earlier, the delivery mechanisms should have been trained to react with greater alacrity. Additionally, alternate mechanisms[319] better

---

[319] Here, given the currency crisis created by demonetization, one wonders whether the Indian Army could have been used to supply currency to various banks and ATM's. The Indian Army is well-known for its ability to manage crisis situations and their integrity is beyond questioning. I am sure that they would have accomplished the task in a much better fashion as compared to the private cash operators, who are prone to corrupt practices at times.

equipped to handle the scale of service and at the required speed should also have been deployed. I would like to believe that the planning bodies and those in charge of execution would be treating this as a learning experience and drawing lessons from it, despite the considerable economic and human cost.

Even while acknowledging the problems associated with the process, **I feel it appropriate to re-emphasize the central theme of this book, which is the need for a forward looking approach to ensure that we maximize the benefits to be had from the demonetization measure, even as we try to minimize the resultant damages.**

Without a doubt, the need of the hour is to jump-start the economy by putting purchasing power back in the hands of the people and by pumping sufficient capital into infrastructure building to generate large scale employment opportunities. These are broad prescriptions of course and I offer below a short list of the specific recommendations[320] made in earlier chapters.

a) Rationalization[321] of income tax and corporate tax through a simple, efficient, self-preserving system with no exemptions. In short, enhance the income tax exemption limit to Rs 10 lakhs per individual and have a flat tax rate of 15 percent on incomes above this limit. This should result in the removal of all discretionary power with the

---

[320] The rationale for these recommendations can be found in the respective chapters given earlier.
[321] See chapter 5 for list of practical steps to be implemented.

income tax officer and a simple, easy to administer tax regime. In addition, corporates should be taxed at 20 percent flat. There should be no exemptions what-so-ever;

b) Reduction[322] of stamp duty to a maximum of 2 percent of the property registration value across states and removal of registration fees across the board. The property guideline value must be commensurately enhanced to reflect the real market values on the ground and specific rules of thumb have been provided in this regard, based on the author's work experience across 570 districts in India;

c) Immediate implementation of the *Lokpal*[323] and *Lokayuktas Act* (2013) along with the enactment of an appropriate legislation for bringing transparency and accountability in public procurement in India;

d) Urgently kick-start growth in several crucial sectors of the economy through implementation of specific proposals[324] for strengthening the key building blocks in the Indian economy—agriculture, manufacturing and services with added emphasis on MSMEs—as well as for providing impetus for rural and urban infrastructure development and engaging with rural/urban communities across India;

---

[322] See chapter 4 for specific action steps.
[323] See chapter 7 for the practical recommendations.
[324] See chapter 6 for a list of the specific proposals.

e) Immediate implementation of reforms vital for cleansing the Indian polity of the bane of corruption and black money; and

f) Last, but not the least, implementation of a range of measures[325] to enhance the inclusiveness, fairness, transparency and accountability of the digital ecosystem in India.

Indeed, in recent weeks, there has been a perceptible shift in the Central Government's demonetization narrative, with the emphasis now on the adoption of digital financial systems. The shift is understandable given that we need to give up our penchant for cash transactions if the economy is to enjoy long-term growth benefits.

Apart from the parallel economy and the shadowy transactions that the usage of cash helps perpetrate, there are also the physical costs involved that we cannot afford to keep underwriting, and at such scale, if we are to grow at a pace and achieve the kind of equitable growth that we aim for. Given that the digital service providers offer far greater ease of access and speed than the formal banks, the thrust on digital financial systems is also understandable.

Equally critical though, is ensuring a safe and smooth transition to the digital economy. While a series of sops had earlier been announced, including waiver of service charges on digital transactions to encourage the shift, the government has recently announced a

---

[325] See chapter 3 for the range of measures suggested.

lucky draw with large cash prizes to retailers/individuals who make the switch to digital financial systems. One must assume that they understand the Indian penchant for incentives.

Even while I have discussed the need to bridge the digital divide in an earlier chapter, I would like to sign off by re-emphasizing on issues related to the switch to the digital economy, given its positioning as the optimal way forward.

First off is the need for an ecosystem that supports the transition to the digital space in a smooth manner. Data connectivity continues to be a challenge in many parts of the country, despite the reported upgrade from 3G to 4G. In the absence of access to the internet, most mobile applications (apps) would be rendered useless. It is critical to ensure data connectivity in every nook and corner of the country, but, equally important is the need to provide backup services in the event of the lack of network access.

Again, continued availability of electricity is also a critical factor. That our systems are not hardy enough to withstand the vagaries of the weather is proven by Chennai's experiences during Cyclone Vardah in December 2016. Even as the city suffered from a lack of access to electricity, data connectivity and even mobile networks, the digital ecosystem completely collapsed, leaving the city's population without any means of transacting, given the already prevalent cash crunch.

The Cinderella Notes

Process and digital literacy is yet another critical need right now. Before we push people headlong into the digital stream, it would be useful if we at least imparted basic survival skills needed to negotiate the new waters and stay afloat. The digital instruments that currently populate the market are designed for those with a fair degree of understanding of both the financial and the digital process. The population that still remains excluded from the formal financial process, and which the country hopes to bring into the digital fold, is not highly literate, both in terms of the process as well as familiarity with the digital space.

There is also the constraint imposed by language. Even if vernacular options are available, the complex language and syntax puts them above the reach of a semi-literate population. Then there is the challenge involved with comprehending the financial transaction process and negotiating its various steps. Clearly, there is a need for process and digital literacy tools and aids, without which it is going to be very difficult for low-income people to use digital finance options. Actual use of these digital finance mechanisms (DFMs) have to be facilitated through applications that handhold the customer and promote digital and process literacy of the end-user in real time, thereby bolstering the use of DFMs.

There are also anti-trust implications that need to be considered in the present scenario. While there are a plethora of players in the digital financial space, there is also scope for monopoly by resorting to unfair trade practises, undercutting opponents and so on.

The Cinderella Notes

The practice of using capital revenues to fund such practices in the form of cash-backs, for example, is not a healthy trend. One must draw a parallel with the situation in the call taxi space in India, where Ola and Uber have more or less driven out the competition by offering superior service at par or even below par prices. The danger is that once they have consolidated their market shares sufficiently, they may jack up prices and the loyal client-base would be forced to continue their patronage, in the absence of viable alternatives. It is important that we guard against the emergence of such a situation in the digital financial services space.

Also important are the unique risks that the digital economy faces, which needs safeguarding against. Unfortunately, no such safeguards exist currently, to the best of my knowledge.[326]. These risks are both known and unknown. Known risks pertain to the safety of digital money, and the experience of Venezuela is a strong case in point. Unknown risks include natural and man-made calamities like the Cyclone Vardah experience referred to earlier. Although it underlined the lack of robustness in our infrastructural systems, it also caught the citizens unaware and resulted in a significant period of hardship when they had no means of making transactions.[327]. The Manipur[328] situation is another

---

[326] See 'Venezuela warns about cybercrime', December 13, 2016, *The Hindu*, Kallol Bhattacherjee,
http://www.thehindu.com/news/national/Venezuela-warns-about-cybercrime/article16801504.ece
[327] See 'No Cash, No Card. How Cyclone Vardah Has Crippled Chennai's Cashless Drive', December 15, 2016, *NDTV*, J Sam Daniel

case in point where the administration has blocked data access with a view to containing riot like situations. Therefore, it is clear that all possible risks associated with the transition to a digital ecosystem need to be thoroughly considered and tackled through an appropriate framework. I would strongly recommend an urgent **yet comprehensive digital ecosystem risk audit**, by an independent agency with no commercial interests in the digital space. The need for an independent third party agency is to avoid conflicts of interests.

In addition, to take care of cyber crime, specialized task forces with qualified people on board—at district and state levels—need to be established. This is to ensure the speedy resolution of criminal cases, especially where consumers have been the victims of cyber crime.

A related issue here is the privacy of data—without a doubt, the digital footprint should not be the cause for creating a security risk for individuals and/or result in the misuse of their personal data. For example, mobile wallets[329] ask for access to a variety of personal data at the time of installation, so much

---

Stalin, http://www.ndtv.com/chennai-news/no-cash-no-card-how-cyclone-vardah-has-crippled-chennais-cashless-drive-1637991

[328] See "Manipur Govt extends suspension of mobile data for another week", December 27, 2016, *The Indian Express*, ANI http://indianexpress.com/article/india/manipur-govt-extends-suspension-of-mobile-data-for-another-week-4446726/

[329] See 'Your digital wallet can be a 'pickpocket'', December 05, 2016, *The Hindu*, Samarth Bansal,
http://www.thehindu.com/news/national/Your-digital-wallet-can-be-a-%E2%80%98pickpocket%E2%80%99/article16760772.ece

of which do not even appear relevant to their purpose. Also, there is no transparency in terms of the exact data being accessed or used, which the consumer is entitled to know. A privacy act with sufficient teeth must, therefore, be enacted immediately to safeguard the data of consumers who leave a digital footprint.

It would serve the transition well in this context, if a Digital Services Consumer Protection Agency (DSCPA) were to be established, on the lines of FINRA[330] (Financial Industry Regulatory Authority), which was established in the United States post the 2008 financial crisis and which has done significant work. The agency could first function as a separate cell under the RBI to look at the above issues and consumer protection aspects in the digital space with a financial exposure, including e-commerce. At a later date, it could be spun off as an independent body with statutory powers.

As part of this, it would also help to have a 24 hour dedicated helpline[331] to redress grievances arising out

---

[330] See http://www.finra.org/

[331] The Government of India's policy think tank, NITI Aayog, along with the *National Association of Software and Services Companies* (NASSCOM, a trade association of Indian Information Technology (IT) and Business Process Outsourcing (BPO) industry and the telecom operators has set up a helpline—14444—to address all queries related to digital payments. See ' Dedicated helpline being set up for digital payments', December 29, 2016, *The Indian Express*, IANS, http://indianexpress.com/article/technology/tech-news-technology/dedicated-helpline-being-set-up-for-digital-payments-4449873/—This is in contrast to the helpline mentioned above—in the text—which is envisaged more as a statutory helpline that can help address consumer grievances.

of digital financial transactions, again, including e-commerce companies. If complaints are not redressed within a maximum period of 24 hours with regard to any refund[332] to be made to the customer"s account, Section 420 under the Indian Penal Code (IPC) should apply to such misdemeanors or oversights on the part of the digital service providers. The DSCPA should also initiate appropriate action separately with regard to such happenings, especially in the case of refunds.

While service charges on digital payment gateways have been waived in the present in a bid to promote digital transacting, it is important that charges on the use of digital finance instruments (Credit Cards at POS, Debit Cards at POS, Mobile Wallets and Prepaid Instruments) are reduced across the board. One way to do it would be to give a holiday to service tax[333] and other charges for these instruments for a period of 3 years. Given the existence of a gender divide in adopting digital financial transaction methods, service tax and other charges should also be waived or reduced significantly for women to encourage them to make the transition to the digital way of transacting. Similarly, merchant acquisition by banks/payment gateways must be facilitated and

---

[332] In some cases, the credit/debit card gets debited but the service is not activated. A classic example is the top up recharge of prepaid mobiles. The refund process normally takes between two to four days (and sometimes even longer), which is unfair as the customer neither has the service nor gets the money back {which is still retained by the digital finance service provider or telecommunications company (TELCO) for a few/several days}.
[333] Or any equivalent tax under the to be implemented GST.

supported as also the setting up of the required acceptance infrastructure.

Finally, it is important that digital service providers (both financial and e-commerce) are subjected to independent periodic audits and are rated in terms of their security measures to protect customer privacy and data. Independent specialized rating agencies may be created, like CRISIL[334] for finance companies and M-CRIL[335] for microfinance institutions, to rate the various risks inherent in the services provided by the Digital Service Providers (DSPs) and their ability to mitigate those, especially from the perspective of protecting customer privacy and data. Such ratings should also provide insight into the ability of the DSP's to manage newer and newer risks occurring in the digital ecosystem, given that technology is often leapfrogged.

Well begun is half done, they say. It is important that due weight is given to all these concerns and the digital ecosystem is empowered upfront to deal with any anomalies that may arise while going forward. Permanent solutions need to found rather than quick fix solutions to any lacunae that may be identified.

The country has been through testing times. Even in the face of adversity, the people have stoically borne inconveniences/losses in the hope of a corruption free economy that will yield benefit to all. There is no denying the benefits that the country would gain

---

[334] See http://www.crisil.com/index.jsp
[335] See http://www.m-cril.com/

from the transition to a less-cash economy, especially in the medium and long term. Hopefully, the government will come up with all the back-up measures needed to tackle the issue of corruption and black money generation and provide the springboard that will not only catapult the economy back on to its feet but also help build a robust digital ecosystem to enable a smooth transition from a 'cash economy' to a 'less-cash economy'.[336]

---

[336] See 'No economy can be fully cashless, it can be 'less cash': Jaitley', December 16, 2016, *The Pioneer,*
http://www.dailypioneer.com/todays-newspaper/no-economy-can-be--fully-cashless-it-can--be-less-cash-jaitley.html

The Cinderella Notes

Appendix 1: Payment System Indicators

Please refer to:
https://rbi.org.in/scripts/BS_ViewBulletin.aspx?Id=166
09, November 10, 2016

Please refer to:
https://rbi.org.in/scripts/BS_ViewBulletin.aspx?Id=159
91, December 10, 2015

The Cinderella Notes

Appendix 2: Digital Solutions

With a view to enabling users to cross barriers imposed by literacy and language and make better use of digital technology to conduct financial transactions, I propose the following products primarily designed to benefit the poor, the rural population and those who continue to remain excluded from the formal financial system.

The first solution is a voice led mobile application that will help users negotiate mobile payment gateways and mobile banking systems, undaunted by language, digital and process literacy. The sections of the population that still remain excluded from the digital financial systems are handicapped by a lack of comprehension of the processes and their working. They need to be imparted digital and process literacy before they can effectively use the available solutions. Yet, given the situation at hand, these users need to be brought up to speed in a hurry. Hence training and educating the users can, at best, be a parallel process and they need to be enabled to get on the digital bandwagon straight up.

It is with a view to making this possible that I propose a voice led mobile app that will hand hold the user through the transaction process. The user will be guided through the various options and screens in the simplest and friendliest manner and the 'virtual voice' will be with him[337] every step of the way, telling him what to do. The mobile app will be location specific and therefore it will choose to speak to the user in the language of the region that he lives in. The option of changing the language to one of his choice will also be afforded to him. Starting with basic financial transactions like sending and receiving

---

[337] Him is used without bias to refer to any person – male/female/other

money, the app will be upgraded to enable the use of more complex functions like bill payments, purchase of train/bus/flight tickets, and even using e-commerce sites.

The Prepaid Debit Cards

Although prepaid debit cards exist in the market from banks such as SBI, IDBI and HDFC, the proposed solution intends to follow the prepaid SIM card model in terms of acquisition and top up of the card balance. It can use the strength of the microfinance sector for its distribution with a techno start-up offering back-end solutions.

The prepaid card can be co-branded by the techno start-up with a nationalized bank and can be made available through the network of microfinance institutions and their field workers. Made available for a minimal entry free, the customer can subsequently keep adding balance to his prepaid card through the deposit of money with the field workers of the microfinance institutions. These field workers will pass on information on the top-up required digitally to the start-up, which will then convey the credit to the cardholder in collaboration with the bank. Appropriate internal control mechanisms will have to be in place during the implementation of this solution. The techno start-up may hold a certain fixed balance with the bank, which can be debited every time the credit needs to be conveyed to the cardholder. The field workers will deposit the cash with the microfinance institutions, which will, in turn, convey the credit to the techno start-up. The cardholders can use the cards at all outlets that accept Visa/Master/RuPay cards and can also withdraw money from ATMs across the country. The techno start-up can be a collaborative venture between the providers of the digital back end solutions, who also undertake distribution responsibilities of the cards, the banks and

The Cinderella Notes

the microfinance network. The cards can be used to issue loans to MSMEs through the SHG network and under the Cooperative/Grameen/MFI model, and also for loan installment collection by the field workers under various options.

Appendix 3: Constitution Amendment Bill for Goods and Services Tax (GST)

The Constitution Amendment Bill for Goods and Services Tax (GST) was approved by The President of India after its passage in the Parliament (Rajya Sabha on 3 August 2016 and Lok Sabha on 8 August 2016) and ratification by more than 50 percent of state legislatures. The Government of India stands committed to replace all the indirect taxes levied on goods and services by the Centre and States and implement GST by April 2017.

GST affords several advantages:

a) With GST, the tax base should become comprehensive as all goods and services will be taxable, with very few exemptions.

b) GST has the potential to be a game changing reform by creating a unified Indian market and thereby, reducing the multiple effect of taxation on the cost of goods and services.

c) GST is sure to have a far-reaching impact on almost all the aspects of the business operations in India, ranging from the pricing of products and services to supply chain management, information technology systems and finance, accounting and legal/tax compliance systems.

While, generally, GST can be considered as good for the country, it should, however, provide special incentives for the adoption of the digital infrastructure.

The Cinderella Notes

Appendix 4: The 2008 Financial Crisis in The United States of America (USA)

If there is one thing that stands out about the 2008 financial crisis in the USA, it is the fact that weak, lax and laissez-faire regulation—caused by lobbying, PACs, campaign financing, and the power of Wall Street to influence policy makers, regulators and others—served as an important factor that triggered the meltdown. There are no two opinions on this and this is what the Financial Crisis Inquiry Commission (FCIC) Final Report[338] dated January 2011 has said over and over again.

If one looks closely at many of the past financial crisis situations (like the 2008 global financial crisis fueled by the U.S. sub-prime and other crisis situations before that), it is clear that they can be linked to lax and laissez-faire regulatory and supervisory frameworks. Frameworks that were either developed by industry insiders with commercial interests or created with significant input from such insiders—both with a view to benefit the overall financial industry concerned.

In other words, these regulatory and supervisory frameworks had serious "conflict of interest situations" that led to such lax and laissez-faire regulatory and supervisory frameworks being developed in the first place. In effect, they were regulating their own industry. There can be no doubt that this was corruption at its worst, caused by inherent conflicts of interests that were at play.

---

[338] Financial Crisis Inquiry Report, Final Report Of The National Commission On The Causes Of The Financial And Economic Crisis In The United States, The Financial Crisis Inquiry Commission, 2011, http://fcic-static.law.stanford.edu/cdn_media/fcic-reports/fcic_final_report_full.pdf

The Cinderella Notes

Despite all that has happened, even today, there is a puzzling lack of attention given to the role played by conflicts of interest in the corruption saga and especially with regard to the larger financial sector. Look at the United Nations Convention Against Corruption (UNCAC). Even the UNCAC only makes a fleeting mention of the role played by conflicts of interests, despite it being the important keystone to unearthing corruption and supporting the structure to fight against corruption worldwide.

It is not just my opinion; many scholars, academics, economists, politicians, and business people worldwide also agree that the close regulation and monitoring of conflicts of interest are of great importance to regulatory ethics. Moreover, this is something that all of us need to note with urgency because, if not eliminated, these conflict of interest situations could spell disaster for the larger financial sector as they will inevitably lead to corruption, and, ultimately, to financial crisis caused by laissez-faire regulation and supervision.

That said, let us now look at what is meant[339] by "conflict of interest." A "conflict of interest" is a conflict between the duty, roles, responsibilities, and private interests of any official that could improperly and unfairly influence the performance of his/her official roles and responsibilities.

By private interests, I mean the following: Private interests include financial, pecuniary and other interests[340]

---

[339] These definitions have been compiled from several sources including OECD and other material found on the web, which are far too numerous to quote. These are gratefully and sincerely acknowledged.
[340] The negotiation of future employment by an official (for himself/family/friends) prior to his leaving his present office is one

which generate a direct personal benefit to the public official as also personal affiliations, associations, and family ties, that could (practically be considered as likely to) improperly and unfairly influence the official's performance of his/her roles, duties and responsibilities.

Defined in this way, conflict of interest has the potential to undermine the proper functioning of institutions (public, private, not-for-profit), governments and the like by:

- Weakening adherence by officials to the ideals of impartiality, objectivity, fairness, and legitimacy, in decision making, and
- Distorting the rule of law, the development and application of policy, the functioning of organizations and markets, as well as the allocation of resources.

Indeed, what is the difference between conflict of interest and corruption?

Conflict of interest situations exist where officials, because of their position, have the *opportunity* to abuse the power and authority of their position for personal and private gain. On the other hand, corruption exists where officials *have abused* their position for personal and private gain. Put differently, conflicts of interest situations do not always lead to corruption. However, where there is corruption, you can be sure that conflicts of interest indeed exist.

---

example here and there are many more examples that I could provide. This is like negotiating a job with a vendor. For example, an official may say, "I will make rules governing X and Y situations very lenient provided you make my nephew the CEO in another project of yours."

The Cinderella Notes

Why do we need to attach so much importance to conflicts of interest with regard to regulation and supervision in the financial sector? Because if conflicts of interest are not eliminated and/or at least properly monitored by independent bodies, or reduced, the situation can easily lead to corruption in regulation and supervision and thereby threaten the entire financial system.

This is not new. This is what past crisis situations have taught us. In fact, if there is a single most recurring theme in financial crises and scandals globally, it is the failure to manage conflicts of interest. The following are some well-known examples.

Let us look this with regard to the larger financial sector in the United States, which provides a very useful lesson with regard to conflicts of interest and their relationship to crisis situations.

As described[341] by former SEC Chairman Arthur Levitt:

> Bank involvement in the securities markets came under close scrutiny after the 1929 market crash. The Pecora hearings of 1933 ...uncovered a wide range of abusive practices on the part of banks and bank affiliates. These included a variety of conflicts of interest; the underwriting of unsound securities in order to pay off bad bank loans; and "pool operations" to support the price of bank stocks.

In fact, as Levitt has further argued,[342] and please note this carefully, it is the significant revelations of

---

[341] Testimony of Arthur Levitt, Chairman U.S. Securities and Exchange Commission,
http://www.sec.gov/news/testimony/testarchive/1995/spch029.txt
[342] Ibid.

The Cinderella Notes

"uncontrolled conflicts of interest" that provided the basis and rationale for the passing of many subsequent regulations—the Securities Act (1933), the Securities Exchange Act (1934), and the Glass-Steagall Banking Act (1933). In fact, it appears that conflicts of interest were also the major reason for the enactment of the Investment Company Act (1940) and the Investment Advisor Act (1940).

Closer to the 1990s, I see numerous examples of conflicts of interest that led directly to the financial crisis:

- The insider trading scandals (such as, the Ivan Boesky and Dennis Levine scandals in the 1980s), the closure of Drexel Burnham Lambert (the investment bank) and the associated (criminal) conviction of its famous employee (Michael Milken) are still fresh in my memory.

- Later, there were more financial scandals in the early 2000s—for example, the internet bubble in 2000/2001 exposed problems with dubious high-flying research analysts (with significant conflicts of interest), whose reports were in fact, influenced by their own institutions' investment banking interests. This, in fact, led to specific provisions in the Sarbanes-Oxley Act that dealt with conflicts of interest among research analysts.

- Then, just over a decade ago, in 2003, the SEC found that the use of brokerage commissions to facilitate the sales of fund shares [was] widespread among funds that relied on broker-dealers to sell fund shares. This led to the adoption of new rules to prohibit funds from this practice.[343]

• Then, even closer to home, we had the mother of all financial crises in recent times—the global financial crisis of 2008—which was again based on significant conflicts of interest in many areas and I quote from the FCIC report hereafter which identifies several key aspects that caused the 2008 financial crisis, including conflicts of interest.

First Cause

The first key point from the FCIC report is given below:

> The captains of finance and the public stewards of our financial system ignored warnings and failed to question, understand, and manage evolving risks within a system essential to the well-being of the American public. Theirs was a big miss, not a stumble. ...

> The prime example is the Federal Reserve's pivotal failure to stem the flow of toxic mortgages, which it could have done by setting prudent mortgage-lending standards. The Federal Reserve was the one entity empowered to do so and it did not. The record of our examination is replete with evidence of other failures: financial institutions made, bought, and sold mortgage securities they never examined, did not care to examine, or knew to be defective; firms depended on tens of billions of dollars of borrowing that had to be renewed each and every night, secured by subprime mortgage securities; and major firms and investors blindly relied on credit rating agencies as their arbiters of risk. What else could one expect on a highway where there were neither

---

[343] Please see: Prohibition on the Use of Brokerage Commissions to Finance Distribution, Investment Company Act Release 26591 (Sept. 2, 2004), 69 Fed. Register 54728, 54728 (Sept. 9, 2004), http://www.sec.gov/rules/final/ic-26591.pdf

speed limits nor neatly painted lines? (FCIC Report, Page no 17)[344]

The reader will note the emphasis on the "pivotal failure" of the regulator—the Federal Reserve. The reader will also note that the FCIC report mentions the fact that:

> Financial institutions made, bought, and sold mortgage securities they never examined, did not care to examine, or knew to be defective; firms depended on tens of billions of dollars of borrowing that had to be renewed each and every night, secured by subprime mortgage securities; and major firms and investors blindly relied on credit rating agencies as their arbiters of risk. (FCIC Report, Page no 17)[345]

And surely, as the FCIC report argues in the next point (given below), law/policy makers and regulators, for reasons best known to them, did have a huge say in creating such a "highway where there were neither speed limits nor neatly painted lines"[346] and where reckless driving was the norm (rather than the exception).

Given the above, you will now understand why it is important that current as well as future law and policy-makers and politicians who participate in the American electoral process, especially for the office of the President of the United States, must come clean on their

---

[344] Financial Crisis Inquiry Report, Final Report Of The National Commission On The Causes Of The Financial And Economic Crisis In The United States, The Financial Crisis Inquiry Commission, 2011, http://fcic-static.law.stanford.edu/cdn_media/fcic-reports/fcic_final_report_full.pdf
[345] Financial Crisis Inquiry Report, Final Report Of The National Commission On The Causes Of The Financial And Economic Crisis In The United States, The Financial Crisis Inquiry Commission, 2011, http://fcic-static.law.stanford.edu/cdn_media/fcic-reports/fcic_final_report_full.pdf
[346] Ibid.

relationships with Wall Street firms. There should be no question about this.

Second Cause

Let us move to the next key point identified by the FCIC:

> We conclude widespread failures in financial regulation and supervision proved devastating to the stability of the nation's financial markets. The sentries were not at their posts, in no small part due to the widely accepted faith in the self-correcting nature of the markets and the ability of financial institutions to effectively police themselves. More than 30 years of deregulation and reliance on self-regulation by financial institutions, championed by former Federal Reserve chairman Alan Greenspan and others, supported by successive administrations and Congresses, and actively pushed by the powerful financial industry at every turn, had stripped away key safeguards, which could have helped avoid catastrophe. This approach had opened up gaps in oversight of critical areas with trillions of dollars at risk, such as the shadow banking system and over-the-counter derivatives markets. In addition, the government permitted financial firms to pick their preferred regulators in what became a race to the weakest supervisor. ...
>
> Changes in the regulatory system occurred in many instances as financial markets evolved. Nevertheless, as the report will show, the financial industry itself played a key role in weakening regulatory constraints on institutions, markets, and products. It did not surprise the Commission that an industry of such wealth and power would exert pressure on policy makers and regulators. From 1999 to 2008, the financial sector expended $2.7 billion in reported federal lobbying expenses; individuals and political action committees in the sector made more than $1 billion in campaign contributions. What troubled us was the extent to which the nation was deprived of the necessary strength and

independence of the oversight necessary to safeguard
financial stability. (FCIC Report, Page no 18)[347]

Please note the comment on the failure of financial
regulation and supervision in causing the crisis as well as
the reference to lobbying expenses, campaign
contributions and the power and wealth of Wall Street to
"exert pressure on policy makers and regulators." For a
moment I thought that it was Bernie Sanders who had
written this report but I was mistaken. These words
appear in the final report of the FCIC, the Statutory
Commission that inquired into the Financial Crisis of
2008. Now, tell me whether, as an American, you feel
comfortable when a potential law/policy maker talks of
reining in Wall Street but refuses to release the paid
speeches that she made to a key Wall Street firm like
Goldman Sachs, which has been repeatedly cited in the
FCIC report.

Third Cause

Alright, let us move on to the next point cited by FCIC
and it is about self-regulation — an idea sold by large
Wall Street Firms, Financial Conglomerates, Big Banks
and Corporations to Law/Policy Makers and Regulators,
who readily bought this idea and faced the consequences
via the financial crisis of 2008:

> We conclude dramatic failures of corporate governance
> and risk management at many systemically important
> financial institutions were a key cause of this crisis. There
> was a view that instincts for self-preservation inside

---

[347] Financial Crisis Inquiry Report, Final Report Of The National
Commission On The Causes Of The Financial And Economic Crisis
In The United States, The Financial Crisis Inquiry Commission,
2011, http://fcic-static.law.stanford.edu/cdn_media/fcic-
reports/fcic_final_report_full.pdf

major financial firms would shield them from fatal risk-taking without the need for a steady regulatory hand, which, the firms argued, would stifle innovation. Too many of these institutions acted recklessly, taking on too much risk, with too little capital, and with too much dependence on short-term funding. In many respects, this reflected a fundamental change in these institutions, particularly the large investment banks and bank holding companies, which focused their activities increasingly on risky trading activities that produced hefty profits. They took on enormous exposures in acquiring and supporting subprime lenders and creating, packaging, repackaging, and selling trillions of dollars in mortgage-related securities, including synthetic financial products. Like Icarus,[348] they never feared flying ever closer to the sun.

Many of these institutions grew aggressively through poorly executed acquisition and integration strategies that made effective management more challenging. The CEO of Citigroup told the Commission that a $40 billion position in highly rated mortgage securities would "not in any way have excited my attention," and the co-head of Citigroup's investment bank said he spent "a small fraction of 1%" of his time on those securities. In this instance, too big to fail meant too big to manage.

Financial institutions and credit rating agencies embraced mathematical models as reliable predictors of risks, replacing judgment in too many instances. Too often, risk management became risk justification.

---

[348] In Greek mythology, Icarus is the son of the master craftsman Daedalus, the creator of the Labyrinth. Icarus and his father attempted to escape from Crete by means of wings that his father had constructed from feathers and wax. Icarus's father warns him first of complacency and then of hubris, asking that he fly neither too low nor too high, so the sea's dampness would not clog his wings or the sun's heat melt them. Icarus ignored his father's instructions not to fly too close to the sun, whereupon the wax in his wings melted and he fell into the sea.

Compensation systems—designed in an environment of cheap money, intense competition, and light regulation— too often rewarded the quick deal, the short-term gain— without proper consideration of long-term consequences. Often, those systems encouraged the big bet—where the payoff on the upside could be huge and the downside limited. This was the case up and down the line—from the corporate boardroom to the mortgage broker on the street.

Our examination revealed stunning instances of governance breakdowns and irresponsibility. You will read, among other things, about AIG senior management's ignorance of the terms and risks of the company's $79 billion derivatives exposure to mortgage-related securities; Fannie Mae's quest for bigger market share, profits, and bonuses, which led it to ramp up its exposure to risky loans and securities as the housing market was peaking; and the costly surprise when Merrill Lynch's top management realized that the company held $55 billion in "super-senior" and supposedly "super-safe" mortgage-related securities that resulted in billions of dollars in losses. (FCIC Report, Page no 18 and 19)[349]

Yet the law/policy makers and regulators swore by self-regulation. Why were they so dogmatic and shortsighted? Self-regulation is an oxymoron and has never worked … ever! It pushes people to fly like Icarus who did not fear flying closer to the sun and simply perished.

Now, this again, is a clear failure on the part of policy and law-makers who were convinced by these large Wall Street firms, financial conglomerates, banks and corporations to bring in the paradigm of self-regulation as

---

[349] Financial Crisis Inquiry Report, Final Report Of The National Commission On The Causes Of The Financial And Economic Crisis In The United States, The Financial Crisis Inquiry Commission, 2011, http://fcic-static.law.stanford.edu/cdn_media/fcic-reports/fcic_final_report_full.pdf

a key component of the regulatory and supervisory process. Again, as before, the cost of this decision was very high and it resulted in the financial crisis of 2008, the impact of which we are still feeling today.

Fourth, Fifth and Sixth Causes

The FCIC report talks of three more critical aspects that led to the financial crisis of 2008 and each of these is highlighted below:

> We conclude a combination of excessive borrowing, risky investments, and lack of transparency put the financial system on a collision course with crisis.
>
> Clearly, this vulnerability was related to failures of corporate governance and regulation, but it is significant enough by itself to warrant our attention here.
>
> In the years leading up to the crisis, too many financial institutions, as well as too many households, borrowed to the hilt, leaving them vulnerable to financial distress or ruin if the value of their investments declined even modestly. For example, as of 2007, the five major investment banks—Bear Stearns, Goldman Sachs, Lehman Brothers, Merrill Lynch, and Morgan Stanley— were operating with extraordinarily thin capital. By one measure, their leverage ratios were as high as 40 to 1, meaning for every $40 in assets, there was only $1 in capital to cover losses. Less than a 3% drop in asset values could wipe out a firm. To make matters worse, much of their borrowing was short-term, in the overnight market—meaning the borrowing had to be renewed each and every day. For example, at the end of 2007, Bear Stearns had $11.8 billion in equity and $383.6 billion in liabilities and was borrowing as much as $70 billion in the overnight market. It was the equivalent of a small business with $50,000 in equity borrowing $1.6 million, with $296,750 of that due each and every day. One can't really ask, "What were they thinking?" when it

seems that too many of them were thinking alike. (FCIC Report, Page no 19 and 20)[350]

Anyone with financial sense will argue that such leverage is ridiculous, and yet it was consciously allowed by the powers that be. Where were regulators and law policy-makers? I don't know. No one seems to know!

> We conclude over-the-counter derivatives contributed significantly to this crisis. The enactment of legislation in 2000 to ban the regulation by both the federal and state governments of over-the-counter (OTC) derivatives was a key turning point in the march toward the financial crisis. ...

> OTC derivatives contributed to the crisis in three significant ways. First, one type of derivative—credit default swaps (CDS)—fueled the mortgage securitization pipeline. CDS were sold to investors to protect against the default or decline in value of mortgage-related securities backed by risky loans. Companies sold protection—to the tune of $79 billion, in AIG's case—to investors in these newfangled mortgage securities, helping to launch and expand the market and, in turn, to further fuel the housing bubble.

> Second, CDS were essential to the creation of synthetic CDOs. These synthetic CDOs were merely bets on the performance of real mortgage-related securities. They amplified the losses from the collapse of the housing bubble by allowing multiple bets on the same securities and helped spread them throughout the financial system.

> Goldman Sachs alone packaged and sold $73 billion in synthetic CDOs from July 1, 2004, to May 31, 2007.

---

[350] Financial Crisis Inquiry Report, Final Report Of The National Commission On The Causes Of The Financial And Economic Crisis In The United States, The Financial Crisis Inquiry Commission, 2011, http://fcic-static.law.stanford.edu/cdn_media/fcic-reports/fcic_final_report_full.pdf

Synthetic CDOs created by Goldman referenced more than 3,400 mortgage securities, and 610 of them were referenced at least twice. This is apart from how many times these securities may have been referenced in synthetic CDOs created by other firms. ...

While financial institutions surveyed by the FCIC said they do not track revenues and profits generated by their derivatives operations, some firms did provide estimates. For example, Goldman Sachs estimated that between 25% and 35% of its revenues from 2006 through 2009 were generated by derivatives, including 70% to 75% of the firm's commodities business, and half or more of its interest rate and currencies business. From May 2007 through November 2008, $133 billion, or 86%, of the $155 billion of trades made by Goldman's mortgage department were derivative transactions.[351] (FCIC Report, Page no 24, 25, 78 and 79)[352]

Here we go once again with another example where regulation was banned *by legislation* and as the FCIC report argues, and I quote, "the enactment of legislation in 2000 to ban the regulation by both the federal and state governments of over-the-counter (OTC) derivatives was a key turning point in the march toward the financial crisis."

Why on earth would the Federal Government ban regulation with legislation and thereby purchase a crisis? The answer eludes me. I simply don't understand why this happened or how it could happen. Was no one watching? Was it lobbying, friendly relationships between

---

[351] FCIC Report (2011), Original Footnote 57: Data provided to the FCIC by Goldman Sachs.
[352] Financial Crisis Inquiry Report, Final Report Of The National Commission On The Causes Of The Financial And Economic Crisis In The United States, The Financial Crisis Inquiry Commission, 2011, http://fcic-static.law.stanford.edu/cdn_media/fcic-reports/fcic_final_report_full.pdf

policy and law-makers with Wall Street firms, paid speeches, and/or campaign donations that did the trick? I'm not sure, and I simply cannot fathom why this banning of regulation happened in the year 2000.

> Removing barriers helped consolidate the banking industry. Between 1990 and 2005, 74 "megamergers" occurred involving banks with assets of more than $10 billion each. Meanwhile, the 10 largest jumped from owning 25% of the industry's assets to 55%. From 1998 to 2007, the combined assets of the five largest U.S. banks—Bank of America, Citigroup, JP Morgan, Wachovia, and Wells Fargo—more than tripled, from $2.2 trillion to $6.8 trillion.[353] And investment banks were growing bigger, too. Smith Barney acquired Shearson in 1993 and Salomon Brothers in 1997, while Paine Webber purchased Kidder, Peabody in 1995. Two years later, Morgan Stanley merged with Dean Witter, and Bankers Trust purchased Alex. Brown & Sons. The assets of the five largest investment banks —Goldman Sachs, Morgan Stanley, Merrill Lynch, Lehman Brothers, and Bear Stearns—quadrupled, from $1 trillion in 1998 to $4 trillion in 2007.[354]

> In the spring of 1996, after years of opposing repeal of Glass-Steagall, the Securities Industry Association—the trade organization of Wall Street firms such as Goldman Sachs and Merrill Lynch—changed course. Because restrictions on banks had been slowly removed during the previous decade, banks already had beachheads in securities and insurance. Despite numerous lawsuits against the Fed and the OCC, securities firms and insurance companies could not stop this piecemeal process of deregulation through agency rulings.[355]

---

[353] FCIC Report (2011), Original Footnote 2: These were the largest banks as of 2007. See FCIC, "Preliminary Staff Report: Too-Big-to-Fail Financial Institutions," August 31, 2010, p. 14.

[354] FCIC Report (2011), Original Footnote 3: Data from SNL Financial (www.snl.com/).

[355] FCIC Report (2011), Original Footnote 12: Securities Industry Association v. Board of Governors of the Federal Reserve System,

Edward Yingling, the CEO of the American Bankers Association (a lobbying organization), said, "Because we had knocked so many holes in the walls separating commercial and investment banking and insurance, we were able to aggressively enter their businesses—in some cases more aggressively than they could enter ours. So first the securities industry, then the insurance companies, and finally the agents came over and said let's negotiate a deal and work together.[356] (FCIC Report, Page no 80, 81 and 82)[357]

In addition, the FCIC Report stated:

The new regime encouraged growth and consolidation within and across banking, securities, and insurance. The bank-centered financial holding companies such as Citigroup, JP Morgan, and Bank of America could compete directly with the "big five" investment banks — Goldman Sachs, Morgan Stanley, Merrill Lynch, Lehman Brothers, and Bear Stearns—in securitization, stock and bond underwriting, loan syndication, and trading in over-the-counter (OTC) derivatives. The biggest bank holding companies became major players in investment banking. The strategies of the largest commercial banks and their holding companies came to more closely resemble the strategies of investment banks. Each had advantages: commercial banks enjoyed greater access to insured deposits, and the investment banks enjoyed less regulation. Both prospered from the late 1990s until the outbreak of the financial crisis in 2007. However,

---

627 F. Supp. 695 (D.D.C. 1986); Kathleen Day, "Reinventing the Bank; With Depression-Era Law about to Be Rewritten, the Future Remains Unclear," *Washington Post*, October 31, 1999.

[356] FCIC Report (2011), Original Footnote 13: Edward Yingling, quoted in "The Making of a Law," *ABA Banking Journal*, December 1999.

[357] Financial Crisis Inquiry Report, Final Report Of The National Commission On The Causes Of The Financial And Economic Crisis In The United States, The Financial Crisis Inquiry Commission, 2011, http://fcic-static.law.stanford.edu/cdn_media/fcic-reports/fcic_final_report_full.pdf

> Greenspan's "spare tire" that had helped make the system less vulnerable would be gone when the financial crisis emerged—all the wheels of the system would be spinning on the same axle. (FCIC Report, Page no 84)[358]

Again, the above represents a classic case where, in the name of innovation and consolidation, regulatory safeguards were removed, resulting in the system being more vulnerable when the financial crisis actually emerged (as all the wheels of the system were indeed spinning on the same axle, which eventually broke under the load). Please note that, as the FCIC report argues very clearly, the financial crisis was essentially caused by a regulatory and policy failure that occurred because regulation and supervision were either lax and/or regulatory safeguards had been removed through lobbying, legislation and the like. We simply cannot afford more of this in the future. That is why, with the backdrop of the 2008 financial crisis (and its aftermath) and the role played by Wall Street (including investment banks, commercial banks, financial conglomerates etc.) in creating and sustaining this crisis, we simply cannot have presidential nominees cozy up to Wall Street and refuse to release transcripts of their paid for speeches. Sorry, but that is unacceptable and is not good electoral governance in any form or manner . . . anywhere!

Seventh Cause

Let's move on further and get to the governance of compensation, which played a very important role in the 2008 financial crisis. Indeed, compensation is one factor

---

[358] Financial Crisis Inquiry Report, Final Report Of The National Commission On The Causes Of The Financial And Economic Crisis In The United States, The Financial Crisis Inquiry Commission, 2011, http://fcic-static.law.stanford.edu/cdn_media/fcic-reports/fcic_final_report_full.pdf

among many that contributed to the financial crisis in the United States, and elsewhere. Moreover, the FCIC report has also mentioned the same and this is quoted below:

> Both before and after going public, investment banks typically paid out half their revenues in compensation. For example, Goldman Sachs spent between 44% and 49% a year between 2005 and 2008, when Morgan Stanley allotted between 46% and 59%. Merrill paid out similar percentages in 2005 and 2006, but gave 141% in 2007—a year it suffered dramatic losses.[359]
>
> As the scale, revenue, and profitability of the firms grew, compensation packages soared for senior executives and other key employees. John Gutfreund, reported to be the highest-paid executive on Wall Street in the late 1980s, received $3.2 million in 1986 as CEO of Salomon Brothers.[360] Stanley O'Neal's package was worth more than $91 million in 2006, the last full year he was CEO of Merrill Lynch.[361] In 2007, Lloyd Blankfein, CEO ofat Goldman Sachs, received $68.5 million;[362] Richard Fuld, CEO of Lehman Brothers, and Jamie Dimon, CEO of JPMorgan Chase, received about $34 million and $28 million, respectively.[363] That year Wall Street paid workers in New York roughly $33 billion in year-end

---

[359] FCIC Report (2011), Original Footnote 63: Goldman Sachs, 2006 and 2009 10-K; Morgan Stanley, 2008 10-K; Merrill Lynch, 2005 and 2008 10-K.

[360] FCIC Report (2011), Original Footnote 64: "Gutfreund's Pay Is Cut," *New York Times,* December 23, 1987.

[361] FCIC Report (2011), Original Footnote 65: Merrill Lynch, "2007 Proxy Statement," p. 38.

[362] FCIC Report (2011), Original Footnote 66: Goldman Sachs, "Proxy Statement for 2008 Annual Meeting of Shareholders," March 7, 2008, p. 16: Blankfein received $600,000 base salary and a 2007 year-end bonus of $67.9 million.

[363] FCIC Report (2011), Original Footnote 67: Lehman Brothers, "Proxy Statement for Year-end 2007," p. 28; JP Morgan Chase, "2007 Proxy Statement," p. 16.

bonuses alone.[364] Total compensation for the major U.S. banks and securities firms was estimated at $137 billion.[365] (FCIC Report, Page no 91)[366]

In effect, in all these firms, the focus was on the short-term performance, incentives, and compensation, when, in reality, the risks (which existed) were mostly, medium and/or long-term. Of course, the regulator and law and policy-makers sat and watched as compensation soared way beyond acceptable levels and firms started paying as high as 50 percent of their revenues in compensation.

Did not the regulators and policy- and law-makers find it strange that:

a) Goldman Sachs spent between 44 per cent and 49 per cent of its revenue per year on compensation (during the years 2005 to 2008);

b) Morgan Stanley allotted between 46 percent and 59 percent; and

c) Merrill paid out similar percentages in 2005 and 2006, and more importantly, gave as high as 141 percent in 2007 (a year in which it suffered dramatic losses).

---

[364] FCIC Report (2011), Original Footnote 68: New York State Office of the State Comptroller, "New York City Securities Industry Bonus Pool," February 23, 2010. The bonus pool is for securities industry (NAICS 523) employees who work in New York City.
[365] FCIC Report (2011), Original Footnote 69: "Banks Set for Record Pay, Top Firms on Pace to Award $145 Billion for 2009, Up 18%, WSJ Study Finds," WSJ.com, January 14, 2010.
[366] Financial Crisis Inquiry Report, Final Report Of The National Commission On The Causes Of The Financial And Economic Crisis In The United States, The Financial Crisis Inquiry Commission, 2011, http://fcic-static.law.stanford.edu/cdn_media/fcic-reports/fcic_final_report_full.pdf

The Cinderella Notes

What on earth were the regulators and policy and law-makers doing? This is where, again, it is very important for a presidential candidate to forego any close relationships with Wall Street. As the 2008 financial crisis has clearly demonstrated, there is no free lunch.

Eighth Cause

As the FCIC report correctly argues, a lot of this happened because conflicts of interest were at play and they were, in a big measure, responsible for the financial crisis of 2008. While there are innumerable examples from the FCIC report that I could cite as evidence of conflicts of interest that were responsible for the financial crisis of 2008, one very relevant example from the SEC[367] is given below:

> Another high profile example of conflict of interest in the recent years is the settlement that the SEC reached with Goldman Sachs, in which that firm paid $550 million to settle charges filed by the Commission, and acknowledged that disclosures made in marketing a subprime mortgage product contained incomplete information as they did not disclose the role of a hedge fund client who was taking the opposite side of the trade in the selection of the CDO.[368]

And I quote:

> Goldman acknowledges that the marketing materials for the ABACUS 2007-ACI transaction contained incomplete information. In particular, it was a mistake for the Goldman marketing materials to state that the reference portfolio was "selected by" ACA Management

---

[367] Carlo V. di Florio, 'Conflicts of Interest and Risk Governance',
U.S. Securities and Exchange Commission, October 22, 2012,
https://www.sec.gov/News/Speech/Detail/Speech/1365171491600
[368] Ibid.

LLC without disclosing the role of Paulson & Co. Inc. in the portfolio selection process and that Paulson's economic interests were adverse to CDO investors. Goldman regrets that the marketing materials did not contain that disclosure.

(http://www.sec.gov/litigation/litreleases/2010/consent -pr2010-123.pdf , Page 2, point 3)

Before I close this appendix, I would like to quote the FCIC report[369] one last time:

Goldman Sachs "Multiplied the Effects of the Collapse in Subprime"

Henry Paulson, the CEO of Goldman Sachs from 1999 until he became secretary of the Treasury in 2006 testified to the FCIC that by the time he became secretary many bad loans already had been issued— "most of the toothpaste was out of the tube"—and that "there really wasn't the proper regulatory apparatus to deal with it."[370] Paulson provided examples: "Subprime mortgages went from accounting for 5 percent of total mortgages in 1994 to 20 percent by 2006. ... Securitization separated originators from the risk of the products they originated." The result, Paulson observed, "was a housing bubble that eventually burst in far more spectacular fashion than most previous bubbles."[371]

---

[369] Financial Crisis Inquiry Report, Final Report Of The National Commission On The Causes Of The Financial And Economic Crisis In The United States, The Financial Crisis Inquiry Commission, 2011, http://fcic-static.law.stanford.edu/cdn_media/fcic-reports/fcic_final_report_full.pdf

[370] FCIC Report (2011), Original Footnote 96: Henry M. Paulson Jr., testimony before the FCIC, Hearing on the Shadow Banking System, day 2, session 1: Perspective on the Shadow Banking System, May 6, 2010, transcript, p. 22.

[371] FCIC Report (2011), Original Footnote 97: Henry M. Paulson Jr., written testimony for the FCIC, Hearing on the Shadow Banking System, day 2, session 1: Perspective on the Shadow Banking System, May 6, 2010, p. 2.

The Cinderella Notes

Under Paulson's leadership, Goldman Sachs had played a central role in the creation and sale of mortgage securities. From 2004 through 2006, the company provided billions of dollars in loans to mortgage lenders; most went to the subprime lenders Ameriquest, Long Beach, Fremont, New Century, and Countrywide through warehouse lines of credit, often in the form of repos.[372] During the same period, Goldman acquired $ 53 billion of loans from these and other subprime loan originators, which it securitized and sold to investors.[373] From 2004 to 2006 Goldman issued 318 mortgage securitizations totaling $184 billion (about a quarter were subprime), and 63 CDOs totaling $32 billion; Goldman also issued 22 synthetic or hybrid CDOs with a face value of $35 billion between 2004 and June 2006.[374] (FCIC Report, Page no 170)

To summarize, the FCIC report cites the following as among the key causes of the financial crisis of 2008:

a) the lack of proper regulation and supervision;

b) the lax and laissez-faire attitude of the regulators and law- and policy-makers (due to conflicts of interests);

c) the reckless ride that many Wall Street firms (including investment banks, commercial banks, financial conglomerates etc.) took off on down a highway with no speed limits;

---

[372] FCIC Report (2011), Original Footnote 98: Goldman Sachs, 2005 and 2006 10-K (appendix 5a to Goldman's March 8, 2010, letter to the FCIC).
[373] FCIC Report (2011), Original Footnote 99: Appendix 5c to Goldman's March 8, 2010, letter to the FCIC.
[374] FCIC Report (2011), Original Footnote 100: Goldman's March 8, 2010, letter to the FCIC, p. 28 (subprime securities).

d) the poor operational practices, weak financial condition, and huge compensation packages at many of these Wall Street firms (including investment banks, commercial banks, financial conglomerates etc.);

e) the conflicts of interest that were prevalent in the larger policy, business, and political environment and so on.

The Cinderella Notes

Appendix 5: The Revolving Door Phenomenon in The United States of America (USA) Prior to the 2008 Financial Crisis

One of the biggest reasons for weak regulatory systems, prior to the 2008 financial crisis, is the near seamless shift of key people from Wall Street and private sector to regulatory and supervisory bodies through the "reverse revolving door" phenomenon.

Top executives of Wall Street firms (and representatives of special interest groups including lobbyists) have been known to take up positions in the Government or the regulatory set up.

Paulson, for example, the Treasury Secretary of the United States during the years 2006–2009 is a classic case. He came to the Treasury after nearly thirty-two years at Goldman Sachs.

Robert Rubin is yet another of those who made the switch from Wall Street to government. It must be recalled here that much of the foundation for the de-regulation that took place during former President Bill Clinton's second term, was laid during Rubin's tenure. It is, of course, common knowledge what this de-regulation ultimately did in terms of repealing the Glass-Steagall Act, thereby resulting in the 2008 financial crisis.[375]

Often called "the reverse revolving door" phenomenon, these people have established a very strong pro-financial sector/Wall Street bias in policy formulation and

---

[375] This is an opinion expressed in the final report of the Financial Crisis Enquiry Commission (FCIC), http://fcic-static.law.stanford.edu/cdn_media/fcic-reports/fcic_final_report_full.pdf

regulatory enforcement by regulators and supervisors that oversee their (former) industry, former employers and/or related institutions. This oftentimes resulted in de-regulation to the detriment of the end user.

Second, is the shift of key people from government institutions to Wall Street and private sector through the normal revolving door phenomenon. There are the cases where key people from regulatory and supervisory bodies and governments have moved (either through a permanent or temporary relationship) to lucrative private-sector positions at Wall Street firms. Two examples are relevant here:

1) Paid speeches delivered by former Government position holders — all the Wall Street speeches by Hillary and Bill Clinton would come under this category; and

2) People like Lawrence Summers, Timothy Geithner, or Robert Rubin for that matter, who, after having served as Treasury Secretary, went on to work with Wall Street firms like D. E. Shaw, Warburg Pincus,[376] and Citigroup respectively.

Third, there have also been situations where former decision makers (including policy makers and executive decision makers) have become paid advocates and use their knowledge of and connections with governmental agencies, regulators, and supervisors to advance the interests of Wall Street companies. This again would be part of Wall Street lobbying. All of these have created significant conflicts of interests prior to the 2008 financial crisis and have been an important reason for the financial crisis having occurred itself.

---

[376] A Wall Street private equity firm

The Cinderella Notes

Appendix 6: The 2010 Andhra Pradesh (AP) Microfinance Crisis: Lessons for Various Stakeholders

Unfortunately, in India, financial inclusion has translated merely to the delivery of consumption credit (and some small production loans). That consumption credit alone is insufficient to reduce or alleviate poverty is perhaps a no-brainer, for all honest development practitioners. Despite the lack of serious impact studies, for those who have worked at the grassroots and continue to so, it is evident that mere access to finance cannot and will not help people come out of poverty. Access to finance is, therefore, best viewed as a necessary, but not sufficient, condition for poverty alleviation.

While microfinance professionals and access to finance enthusiasts can perhaps take comfort in the fact that consumption loans alone cannot make a dent on poverty, there is a caveat in order. They cannot escape the fact that the drive and desire to include low-income people with regard to financial services has resulted in the proliferation of financial services focused on loans and even within loans, primarily consumption lending. The enthusiasm to include low-income people has also led to not-so-good practices including multiple lending, over-lending, top-up loans, ghost/*benami* loans, and the like; driven by the motivation of some MFIs to generate huge wealth for themselves and their promoters.

In fact, one of the major reasons for the 2010 AP microfinance crisis was the mindless drive to include people financially, without asking the question(s) on whether the current bouquet of financial services being offered were indeed appropriate, whether the practices being followed were fair, transparent, legal and ethically sound, and whether the other conditions so necessary for

228

effective use of the financial services existed at the grassroots.

Specifically, while MFIs grew for different reasons, it was during this period of burgeoning growth (April 2008–March 2010 and thereafter until September 2010) that the hitherto highly successful model of JLGs/centres was severely diluted. And the changes did more harm than good to the original concept of joint liability and peer pressure—as several JLGs operated in a mutually reinforcing (cartel-like) manner within a centre.

Four issues are relevant here:

- One: The normal and established processes of client acquisition through green field methods—where MFIs laboriously promoted their own groups, nurtured them and painstakingly created a culture of credit discipline and high repayment based on mutual trust and other aspects—were slowly abandoned by many MFIs because of their urgency to grow fast. Process mapping, which is a good tool by itself, and efficiency goals, which are laudable, were erroneously used to quicken client acquisition strategies and other related processes. Thus, an undue emphasis was placed on quicker identification of clients, faster processing of loan applications, and so on. And basic issues such as the understanding of a client's antecedents and contextual situations, preparation of clients, analysis of client/household loan absorption and debt-servicing capacity and the like—which were the hallmarks of the green field client-acquisition strategy in the traditional Grameen model—were slowly but surely ignored and bypassed.

- Two: Given that clients needed to be identified faster and loans disbursed to them quickly, the MFIs concerned had just two options for client acquisition: (i) acquisition—whereby MFIs started taking over the portfolio of smaller MFIs or specific JLGs. Sometimes, SHGs were also taken over (cannibalized) and split into several JLGs (depending on the size of SHG); and (ii) mutual sharing—whereby several MFIs decided to share and use their available JLGs/clients on successive days and on the basis of a simple reciprocal arrangement. While both strategies were used, over time, cartels of MFIs started to follow the latter as it was a win-win situation for all of them.

• Three: Both of these led to the emergence of power brokers (also called broker agents[377] or ring leaders)—they were basically centre leaders (or sometimes, even group leaders, loan officers, and local political honchos) who had access to a captive set of JLGs and clients. These new intermediaries started to match-make with different MFIs on increasingly attractive and exploitative terms. Thus, slowly, these agents became the most powerful pivot in the local microfinance system and various processes were

---

[377] (a) Implementation safeguards against notorious agents are an imperative for the proposed microfinance bill (http://www.moneylife.in/article/implementation-safeguards-against-notorious-agents-are-an-imperative-for-the-proposed-microfinance-bill/19017.html) by Ramesh S. Arunachalam, August 18, 2011; (b) How and why did microfinance agents become a part of the Indian microfinance business? (http://www.moneylife.in/article/how-and-why-did-microfinance-agents-become-a-part-of-the-indian-microfinance-business/19301.html) by Ramesh S. Arunachalam, August 29, 2011; and (c) Implementation safeguards against notorious agents are an imperative for the proposed microfinance bill (http://www.moneylife.in/article/implementation-safeguards-against-notorious-agents-are-an-imperative-for-the-proposed-microfinance-bill/19017.html) by Ramesh S. Arunachalam, August 18, 2011.

outsourced to them, often without any quality checks. The outsourced processes ranged from client acquisition to KYC documentation, loan disbursement, repayment collection, and so on. Over time, this outsourcing through agents became an established strategy and the agents became omnipresent and omnipotent in the Indian microfinance industry. They often demanded their pound of flesh and got it, too. It appears that the coercive practices and multiple lending, which have often been cited in the 2010 AP crisis, were due to the presence and use of such agents. It is also clear that, given the burgeoning growth and prevalence of such agent-led decentralized microfinance models, it would be difficult to enforce concepts like social performance[378] on the ground.

- Four: Over the period April 2008–March 2010 and thereafter, growth did not come from adding fresh clients. Rather, it came through concurrent loans (from the same MFI) to its clients and multiple lending[379] to shared JLGs/clients, who were serviced by different MFIs on different days. In fact, data reveal that for the six large AP-headquartered NBFC MFIs, while their clients grew by about 1.30 times across two reference periods (April 2008–March 2009 and April 2009–March 2010), the growth in gross loan portfolio across these two periods was about 2.19[380] times, indicating that portfolio deepening had

---

[378] Microfinance: Will seal of excellence and social performance management as yardsticks work?, Ramesh S Arunachalam, September 24, 2011, http://www.moneylife.in/article/microfinance-will-seal-of-excellence-and-social-performance-management-as-yardsticks-work/20038.html

[379] Also ghost lending.

[380] This should have been higher at 2.47 had the Mix Market retained the original GLP figures that it had put out in 2010/2011 for BASIX

occurred perhaps through larger or successive or multiple loans to the clients.

These concurrent and parallel MFI loans, through shared JLGs and clients, appeared to be a godsend and clients just grabbed them during the phase of burgeoning growth—as by then many of them realized that they could not service their increasing debt. The cases of Zaheera Bhee[381] and others clearly illustrate this. The MFIs too were ecstatic about turbo charging financial inclusion and so were equity investors, banks, regulators/supervisors, policymakers, and other stakeholders including international bodies such as the CGAP. This is a critical point that needs to be noted. The outreach of the Indian microfinance industry even today needs significant correction and revision to reflect this reality of concurrent loans, ghost loans and multiple loans to shared JLGs/clients.

Therefore, it is high time that we recognize and use the following lessons (from the Indian microfinance crisis) with regard to promoting inclusive finance for low-income people, in India and globally:

Lesson # 1: The scope of current inclusive finance practice in India is rather narrow. While the intentions (like the report of the Financial Inclusion Committee and other policy pronouncements) may have been to provide

---

and SHARE. For some reason, Mix Market changed its original figures for BASIX and SHARE respectively from US$ 223,229,799 and US$ for 490,923,201 to US$ 172,484,946 and US$ 376,593,362. I have the original print screen data and other pieces of evidence with regard to the original data put out by Mix Market. There are several other issues with the Mix Market database and I can provide the details if required.
[381]http://microfinance-in-india.blogspot.com/2010/11/can-we-bring-back-ayeshas-ammy.html

low-income clients with access to a wide range of need-based financial services, in reality, the inclusive finance (or financial inclusion) paradigm[382] has mainly led to the proliferation of credit and primarily, consumption loans, although there have been some small production/livelihood loans.

Lesson # 2: Standard (MFI) loans for consumption and/or small production needs, which dominate microfinance (or access to finance) in India today, tend to work well for loan sizes in the range of Rs. 10,000–Rs. 15,000 per client and at most <= Rs. 50,000.

Lesson # 3: Rs. 50,000 as the loan amount is some sort of *Lakshman Reka,*[383] that the MFIs should not breach, unless they are absolutely sure of the individual/household having the requisite debt servicing ability (could be a livelihood, production unit, and/or labour, etc.) to repay the larger loan. This is the most important lesson from the 2010 AP crisis for MFIs, banks, policymakers, regulators/supervisors, and other stakeholders.

Lesson # 4: Indiscriminate (and multiple) lending to low-

---

[382]In India, typically, financial inclusion (FI) is presently characterized by (i) preoccupation with opening of savings accounts; (ii) large focus on consumption credit and small production loans; (iii) low outreach with regard to vulnerable groups in agriculture; (iv) lack of suitable and affordable risk management services; and (v) lack of appropriate livelihood financing. The two aspects of lack of suitable and affordable risk management services and lack of appropriate and affordable livelihood financing are noteworthy aspects because they again show the huge gaps between a great vision and intended strategy (the recommendation of the well-intentioned Financial Inclusion Committee) and actual implementation on the ground, which is narrowly focused on consumption and small production credit.

[383]A popular metaphor for a line not to be crossed.

income people under the pretext of furthering financial inclusion—without regard to their (and their families) loan absorption and debt servicing capacity, and especially in the wake of vulnerable livelihoods, can only prove to be a recipe for disaster. As has been demonstrated by the 2010 AP crisis, this will ultimately exclude them altogether from the financial system. As has been argued, when people with weak and vulnerable livelihoods are loaned large sums of money (> Rs. 50,000), repayment will either have to come from fresh loans (i.e., greening through concurrent/multiple lending) and/or restructuring of loans. At some point, this cycle will (have to) stop and the bubble will simply burst. These clients will then become financially excluded all over again.

If that is the scenario, what can nodal institutions do to help the microfinance industry overcome this precarious situation? First, they can help re-engineer the financial inclusion paradigm, to address some of the issues mentioned here. In my opinion, this reengineering should ensure the delivery of quality credit that will reduce risk and vulnerability of low-income clients and give them more choices.[384]

By quality credit, I am arguing for a greater focus on post-harvest and/or post-production financing for agriculture and other sectors that provide (or can provide) significant livelihoods opportunities for low-income people.

In other words, among other things, this would call for the financing of agriculture produce/other products[385] marketing—a very critical aspect for small/marginal

---

[384]This can happen through alternative channels that afford lower costs, have greater trust, and high levels of mutual acceptance.
[385]Like handicrafts, etc.

producers[386] as it has the potential to enhance choices for them in terms of buyers, and so on.

Of course, here, the existing relationships would need to be better understood if financial products are to be developed and delivered through appropriate channels.[387] Second, these nodal agencies must ensure that the focus of financial inclusion is reengineered such that the delivery of a wide range of financial services (loans, savings, insurance, pensions, etc.) are used strategically to drive higher rewards, better remuneration, and greater power down the value chain—otherwise, it will be of limited use.

Hence, they need to help initiate a new microfinance paradigm[388] where financial products, mechanisms, and instruments can be used to perform the following:

- Reduce risk/vulnerability[389] in the existing livelihoods of low-income people, arising from various market imperfections—examples include warehouse receipt financing implemented with appropriate safeguards, pro-poor value -chain financing, and so on;

- Help create strong safety and security nets[390] for these low-income clients for a range of aspects

---

[386]MSMEs as well.

[387]And tThis would need to be validated specifically for a context, a product, and a partner but these are general suggested arrangements.

[388]Source: Adapted from Arunachalam, Ramesh S, "UNDP Financial Inclusion Strategy in 7 Focus States: Strategic Consideration and Suggestions, UNDP," 2007.

[389]Weather and crop insurance are gaining ground. Contract farming schemes exist but are not producer oriented.

[390]Some innovations exist here for health as well as life coverage but much work is necessary in the nature of product design and also distribution. Micro-pension schemes are also available.

including various insurance and risk mitigation products;

- Enable these low-income clients to pursue diversified/migratory livelihoods where required;

- Facilitate re-inclusion of these low-income people (who were once included but subsequently excluded because of fragile livelihoods); and

- Create risk management mechanisms[391] to ensure that they continue to stay financially included, in the context of their fragile livelihoods.

Thus, I would very much like the nodal agencies to champion the larger cause of reengineering the financial inclusion paradigm to facilitate poverty alleviation on the ground. I am sure they have the wherewithal and resources to do this. Let us hope their governance structure and senior management take this appeal seriously and demonstrate sufficient will to do this in real time, on the ground.

Interestingly, much of what happened in Andhra Pradesh in 2010 is now replicating itself in other states of India. Whether a pan India microfinance crisis will unfold or not, is an aspect that time alone can answer!

---

[391]Post harvest loans in fisheries/agriculture and warehouse receipts are examples of such products.

Appendix 7: Voluntary Income Disclosure Scheme of The Internal Revenue Service (IRS) in the United States of America (USA)

IRS Makes Changes to Offshore Programs; Revisions Ease Burden and Help More Taxpayers Come into Compliance[392]

IR-2014-73, June 18, 2014

WASHINGTON — The Internal Revenue Service announced today major changes in its offshore voluntary compliance programs, providing new options to help both taxpayers residing overseas and those residing in the United States. The changes are anticipated to provide thousands of people a new avenue to come into compliance with their U.S. tax obligations.

The changes include an expansion of the streamlined filing compliance procedures announced in 2012 and important modifications to the 2012 Offshore Voluntary Disclosure Program (OVDP). The expanded streamlined procedures are intended for U.S. taxpayers whose failure to disclose their offshore assets was non-willful.

"This opens a new pathway for people with offshore assets to come into tax compliance," said IRS Commissioner John Koskinen. "The new versions of our offshore programs reflect a carefully balanced approach to ensure everyone pays their fair share of taxes owed. Through the changes we are announcing today, we provide additional flexibility in key respects while

---

[392] Source: 'IRS Makes Changes to Offshore Programs; Revisions Ease Burden and Help More Taxpayers Come into Compliance', IR-2014-73, June 18, 2014, https://www.irs.gov/uac/newsroom/irs-makes-changes-to-offshore-programs-revisions-ease-burden-and-help-more-taxpayers-come-into-compliance

maintaining the central components of our voluntary programs."

Balanced against the modified programs is the government's ongoing effort to combat the misuse of offshore assets. The IRS, working closely with the U.S. Department of Justice, continues to investigate foreign financial institutions that may have assisted U.S. taxpayers in avoiding their tax filing and payment obligations. In addition, on July 1, the new information reporting regime resulting from the Foreign Account Tax Compliance Act (FATCA) will go into effect. Thousands of foreign financial institutions will begin to report to the IRS the foreign accounts held by U.S. persons.

The current Offshore Voluntary Disclosure Program was launched in 2012 and is the successor to prior voluntary programs offered in 2011 and 2009. Since the launch of the first program, more than 45,000 taxpayers have come into compliance voluntarily, paying about $6.5 billion in taxes, interest and penalties.

The expansion of the streamlined procedures and modifications to OVDP reflect the thoughtful input of the tax community given the growing awareness among U.S. taxpayers of their offshore tax obligations.

"Through our enforcement efforts and implementation of FATCA, taxpayers are more aware of their obligations, and we believe want to come into compliance," Koskinen said. "In this rapidly changing environment, we listened to feedback from the tax community as well as the National Taxpayer Advocate about our voluntary programs. We have made important adjustments to provide opportunities for all U.S. taxpayers to come in, including those who are not willfully hiding assets."

The Cinderella Notes

Streamlined Procedures Expanded

The changes announced today make key expansions in the streamlined procedures to accommodate a wider group of U.S. taxpayers who have unreported foreign financial accounts.

The original streamlined procedures announced in 2012 were available only to non-resident, non-filers. Taxpayer submissions were subject to different degrees of review based on the amount of the tax due and the taxpayer's response to a "risk" questionnaire.

The expanded streamlined procedures are available to a wider population of U.S. taxpayers living outside the country and, for the first time, to certain U.S. taxpayers residing in the United States. The changes include:

☞ Eliminating a requirement that the taxpayer have $1,500 or less of unpaid tax per year;

☞ Eliminating the required risk questionnaire;

☞ Requiring the taxpayer to certify that previous failures to comply were due to non-willful conduct.

For eligible U.S. taxpayers residing outside the United States, all penalties will be waived. For eligible U.S. taxpayers residing in the United States, the only penalty will be a miscellaneous offshore penalty equal to 5 percent of the foreign financial assets that gave rise to the tax compliance issue.

The Cinderella Notes

Offshore Voluntary Disclosure Program (OVDP) Modified

The changes announced today also make important modifications to the OVDP. The changes include:
- ☞ Requiring additional information from taxpayers applying to the program;
- ☞ Eliminating the existing reduced penalty percentage for certain non-willful taxpayers in light of the expansion of the streamlined procedures;
- ☞ Requiring taxpayers to submit all account statements and pay the offshore penalty at the time of the OVDP application;
- ☞ Enabling taxpayers to submit voluminous records electronically rather than on paper;
- ☞ Increasing the offshore penalty percentage (from 27.5% to 50%) if, before the taxpayer's OVDP pre-clearance request is submitted, it becomes public that a financial institution where the taxpayer holds an account or another party facilitating the taxpayer's offshore arrangement is under investigation by the IRS or Department of Justice.

Statement of IRS Commissioner John Koskinen[393]
June 18, 2014

Today we're announcing a number of important changes to our offshore account compliance program that we believe will lead to a significant increase in the number of U.S. taxpayers coming forward to report on undisclosed foreign accounts.

---

[393] Source: Statement of IRS Commissioner John Koskinen, June 18, 2014, https://www.irs.gov/uac/newsroom/statement-of-irs-commissioner-john-koskinen

The Cinderella Notes

The steps we're outlining today include an expanded streamlined filing compliance process and important modifications to our Offshore Voluntary Disclosure Program, or OVDP. The combined effect of these revisions will be to allow more taxpayers to participate. This reflects a carefully balanced approach. We are providing additional flexibility in key parts of our compliance effort while maintaining central components of the offshore program.

Our goal is to build on the success the IRS has already had in reducing offshore tax evasion through the OVDP, which allows individuals to avoid criminal prosecution if they disclose their foreign accounts and pay a substantial penalty. The current OVDP is the successor to prior initiatives in 2011 and 2009. Taken together, these programs have resulted in more than 45,000 disclosures and the collection of about $6.5 billion in taxes, interest and penalties. To supplement the OVDP, in 2012 we added what we call the streamlined filing compliance procedures. This has provided a way for a limited group of U.S. taxpayers living abroad who didn't know they were out of compliance to catch up on their U.S. filing requirements without paying steep penalties.

We are announcing two sets of actions. These involve some very technical issues, but they carry great importance for thousands of taxpayers and our continuing efforts in the offshore arena.

First, we're expanding the streamlined procedures to cover a much broader group of U.S. taxpayers we believe are out there who have failed to disclose their foreign accounts but who aren't willfully evading their tax obligations. To encourage these taxpayers to come forward, we're expanding the eligibility criteria, eliminating a cap on the amount of tax owed to qualify for the program, and doing away with a questionnaire that applicants were required to complete.

Second, we will be reshaping the terms for taxpayers to participate in the OVDP. This is designed to cover those whose failure to comply with reporting requirements is considered willful in nature, and who therefore don't qualify for the streamlined procedures. These changes will help focus this program on people seeking certainty and relief from criminal prosecution. From now on, people who want to participate in this program will have to provide more information than in the past, submit all account statements at the time they apply for the program, and in some cases pay more in penalties than they would have done had they entered this program earlier.

These changes reflect the helpful feedback of tax practitioners and the National Taxpayer Advocate, along with what we learned in our experience operating the OVDP. Over time, we discovered that there were people, including many here in the U.S., for whom the existing program penalties were too harsh or restrictive. These people had small enough issues that they didn't really need the protection from criminal prosecution offered by the OVDP. But they also didn't fit into the narrow criteria of the streamlined procedures, either.

It's important to keep in mind that the IRS is seeking a balanced approach with this program, particularly in light of our other work on offshore issues. Our aim is to get people to disclose their accounts, pay the tax they owe and get right with the government. At the same time, for important categories of these non-willful people with offshore issues, a compliance regime that is too harsh won't net the desired result.

The Cinderella Notes

In addition, we want to send a message to anyone who continues to willfully and aggressively evade our tax laws by hiding money overseas that they will pay a higher price for that noncompliance. Even though we're tightening components of the OVDP, we still believe it's a better deal than the alternative, because if we find you, you will face higher penalties and, as the record shows, could face criminal prosecution and jail time.

We want everyone to know that we are continuing our efforts to track down people still out there who are hiding assets overseas. More information on these accounts is coming in every day. For example, Swiss banks are cooperating through a program put in place last year by the Department of Justice. I would note that Justice recently reached an historic agreement with Credit Suisse. Also, more banks around the world will be coming forward with information on their U.S. customers beginning July 1. That's when reporting requirements under the Foreign Account Tax Compliance Act, or FATCA, go into effect. It's clear that the days of hiding assets in accounts overseas are coming to an end. There is no reason not to come into compliance.

We encourage taxpayers who are concerned about their undisclosed offshore accounts to come in voluntarily before learning that the U.S. is investigating the bank or banks where they hold accounts. By then, it will be too late to avoid the new higher penalties under the OVDP of 50 percent – nearly double the regular 27.5 percent.

For anyone who wants to come into compliance but isn't sure what to do, I recommend talking to a tax professional or going to our website, IRS.gov. This has a wealth of information about what disclosures are required and how to make them; we plan to add to this area.

For me as a tax administrator, the bottom line on what we're announcing today is about fairness. For our system of voluntary tax compliance to work right, the average taxpayer who abides by the law has to be confident that everyone is being held to a similar standard. As part of that, people can no longer expect to hide their money in foreign countries and avoid paying their fair share.

2012 Offshore Voluntary Disclosure Program[394]

The IRS Offshore Voluntary Disclosure Program is working with taxpayers whose penalties may be reduced. The IRS began an open-ended OVDP in January 2012 because of strong interest in the 2009 and 2011 programs. The IRS may end the 2012 program at any time in the future.

The IRS is offering taxpayers with undisclosed income from offshore accounts another opportunity to get current with their tax returns. The 2012 OVDP has a higher penalty rate than the previous programs, but offers clear benefits to encourage taxpayers to disclose foreign accounts now rather than risk detection by the IRS and possible criminal prosecution.

This is a continuation of the program's modified terms introduced in 2012. For purposes of referring to this modified program, it may be referred to as the 2014 OVDP. The modifications are effective on July 1, 2014.

In addition to the OVDP, we offer additional options available to U.S. taxpayers with undisclosed foreign financial assets.

---

[394] Source: 2012 Offshore Voluntary Disclosure Program, https://www.irs.gov/uac/2012-offshore-voluntary-disclosure-program

The Cinderella Notes

2009 Offshore Voluntary Disclosure Program[395]

Update Aug. 31, 2011 — MEMORANDUM *FOR ALL OVDI EXAMINERS (Use of Discretion on 2009 OVDP Cases, dated March 1, 2011) has been added under Related Items at the bottom of this page.*

*The 2009 Offshore Voluntary Disclosure Program ended on Oct. 15, 2009. However, the new 2011 Offshore Voluntary Discllcosure Initiative was announced on Feb. 8 and runs through Aug. 31, 2011. For more information about the 2011 initiative, visit (*2011 OVDI landing page*) for general information on the IRS's voluntary disclosure program, visit the voluntary disclosure page.*

Taxpayers with unreported income relating to offshore transactions who wish to voluntarily disclose the information to the IRS can find information on the process.

For a complete understanding of the voluntary disclosure procedures, see Internal Revenue Manual (IRM) 9.5.11.9

Taxpayers wanting to participate in the IRS voluntary disclosure process should call the phone number associated with the state in which they reside. See Contact IRS About Voluntary Disclosure. (updated 02/08/2011)

On September 21, 2009, the IRS announced a one-time extension of the September 23, 2009, deadline for special voluntary disclosures by taxpayers with unreported

---

[395] Source: 2009 Offshore Voluntary Disclosure Program, https://www.irs.gov/uac/2009-offshore-voluntary-disclosure-program

income from hidden offshore accounts. Taxpayers now have until October 15, 2009. There will be no further extensions.

The September 23, 2009, deadline for certain FBAR filers and certain offshore-related information returns who have no unreported income is also extended to October 15, 2009. All other guidance included below may still be relied upon.

Appendix 8: Financial Inclusion of Sugarcane Farmers in Modern-day India

In some ways, financing arrangements today penalize the small producer for mistakes of other parties. There is an urgent need to make financial products for low-income people client-sensitive and responsive.

Even as the drive to enhance financial inclusion continues, there are very small things, which if done, can stabilize the inclusion of a large number of low-income people (farmers) and prevent them from being excluded again.

Let me start with an example and I hope that commercial banks and (any) microfinance institutions (MFIs) involved in this space attempt to redress the same. I also hope that the Reserve Bank of India (RBI) looks into this issue so that the tripartite contract farming products become more sensitive to the needs of low-income clients and are fair to them. And while the problems described affect all farmers, the effect on marginal/small farmers is much higher as they do not have diversified sources of income.

Specifically, I take the case of sugarcane farming, and illustrate the need for available financial products to be made more client-sensitive and responsive. Financial inclusion of sugarcane farmers[396] is typically undertaken through contract farming in India, with tripartite agreements between banks/MFIs, sugar factories and clients. While the banks/MFIs are the real drivers of this financial inclusion arrangement, often, the sugar factories,

---

[396] There are said to be over 40 million Sugarcane farmers in India and another 50 million people are supposedly dependent on this industry for their livelihoods.

which provide the inputs and technical assistance, also play an important role.

Consider a marginal sugarcane farmer like Ramaiah (in Madurai district) who has two acres of land. The story of Ramaiah symbolizes what a typical small sugarcane farmer goes through. Ramaiah was financially included when the cane supervisor in a major sugar factory approached him in 2007 and asked him to grow sugarcane in one and a half acres of his two acre land with a perennial well. Under this supposedly inclusive tripartite contract farming arrangement (between farmer, sugar factory and bank), the factory was to supply the inputs, provide technical assistance and buy back the sugarcane,; the bank to provide the loan for buying the inputs, including seeds and fertilizers, and the farmhands to cultivate the crop and earn returns.

Ramaiah was a small farmer who grew vegetables and the family labour of four people was sufficient to get out the vegetables in time and to the nearby town market. While Ramaiah did not make much money from vegetables the year around, there was at least one season in a year where he would reap bumper returns - due to marriages being plentiful, lower produce coming to the vegetable market during the period of heavy rains in October/November and other factors.

Ramaiah was clearly sold on the sugarcane idea suggested by the cane supervisor of a sugar factory, who had argued that the sugarcane crop (and intercrop of onions) could help him generate handsome returns. But alas, that was not to be and Ramiah"s experience with sugarcane farming, as that of many (small/marginal) farmers across the country, was one of complete disaster. Having received a bank loan, he barely managed to get any money, post harvest, from the first sugar crop. The ratoon crops were bigger disasters in subsequent years, and today, the bank is proceeding against him for recovery of dues and he is excluded from the financial system, as are many others like him who took to sugarcane farming.

What are the causes for this? Ramaiah says that the whole tripartite (financial) inclusion arrangement is structured against farmers, like him, for several reasons.

First, the sugarcane setts (seeds) supplied to him (as part of the loan) were over-mature and hence, germinations were low and a lot of gap filling[397] had to be done. Ramaiah asks, why should I pay for gap filling when poor sugar setts were supplied by the sugar factory in the first place?[398]

To understand this, consider the following example. Normally 35,000 sugarcane setts can be planted in one acre of land. Assuming a germination of 60 percent, the farmer will have to gap fill the remaining 40 percent setts again, if he/she is to get a decent yield. The population is the key to getting a good yield; but to maintain the population,[399] the farmer has to gap fill and often

---

[397] This would include cost of the replacement seeds and labour for planting these.

[398] The sugar factory has control of the sugarcane setts supplied as it cuts the standing sugarcane from (other farmer) fields specified as sugar setts (seeds).

[399] For example, 35000 sugarcane setts are typically planted in an acre. Each sett has 2 eyes and this makes it 70,000 eyes in 1 acre of land. Each eye grows to become a shoot weighing approximately 1 kilo in 11/12 months, depending on the variety. If 70,000 eyes germinate (100% germination) and each of them reaches 1 kilo in 11/12 months, then the farmer gets a yield of 70 tonnes per acre. If there is 60% germination, then the yield is 42 tonnes per acre (70000 setts x 60% germination x 1 kilo = 42 tonnes) and so on. Therefore,

unilaterally bear the cost. And more often than not, for a variety of reasons beyond the farmer's control, the setts supplied do not germinate fully.

As part of the arrangement in contract farming, the farmer gap fills the sugarcane setts (in case of poor germination) and he/she bears the cost of poorly germinating seeds, which is typically added to the loan. Thus, the farmer bears the burden despite the fact that poor germination often occurs because poor setts were supplied by the sugar factory {mainly due to the supply of more than mature setts, or immature setts, or setts from a ratoon (2nd cycle) sugarcane crop and often caused by factors beyond the farmer's control}.

Please note the fact that the cost of gap filling is always invariably borne by the small producer, even if poor seeds (setts) have been supplied by the sugar factory. The sugar factory is the key player here because it decides which farmer's crop will go for seed, when it will be cut and supplied and so on. Therefore, under the tripartite financial inclusion (FI) arrangement, the onus for the quality of setts (seeds) is almost entirely that of the sugar factory.

A **second** reason Ramaiah mentioned was the lack of fertilizers, microbes (like Rhizobium) and tonics on time, which meant there were huge delays in fertilizer application. Ramaiah argues that, as he found out later, while the complete loan interest ticks away from the date of signing the agreement with the bank/sugar factory, the supply of ingredients (included in the loan) by the factory is neither on time, nor of specified quality. He argues that, time is of the essence in sugarcane farming and when that

---

maintaining the sugar sett population, at a high and optimal level, is crucial to getting a good yield.

critical time is passed, no matter how much extra fertilizer is given, the growth of the crop will falter. He also complains he had to do extra weeding before the late fertilizer application as weeds had grown again in the intervening period.

A **third** issue he mentions is that sugarcane must be cut at the appropriate time, and here again, there are delays in cutting orders from the sugar factory. In his case, he argues that the cane was cut when it was overripe, and hence, there was a huge loss to him. He argues that undesirable practices prevail here and those who pay a bribe get their cutting orders earlier.

A **fourth** reason is the aspect of cut cane being lifted after a significant delay, as a result of which the cane weight comes down and there is a loss to the farmer. He argues that nefarious practices in transportation effectively increase the lead time from when the cane is cut, to when the cane is transported and delivered to the factory. In his case, the cut cane was allowed to lie on the ground for over two days and this meant moisture loss (and perhaps sugar content) as a result of which there is was considerable weight loss and consequent yield and revenue loss for the small farmer. In fact, he cites that this is a very serious problem for small farmers as the contractors arranged by the sugar factory for transporting the cane from the farmer"s field to the sugar factory insist on bribes/bata and *"baksheesh"* to lift the cane. If farmers do not comply, they leave the cut cane to dry in the field and this can seriously reduce the yield and resultant return for the farmers.

Likewise, there are many other instances of problem situations in sugarcane cultivation, where marginal/ small farmers are hit quite badly. The larger point is just a simple one—the financial product is simply not sensitive to the needs of the small farmer and it perhaps even penalizes him/her for the "wrong doing" of other parties. Poor seed supplied by the sugar factory could cause lower germination, but gap filling cost is always that of the farmer. The machines in the sugar factory could have been stopped (due to failure/fault) and as a result, the cane of the small farmer cannot be unloaded and thus, not weighed at all - —there are many cases, where the small farmer has lost almost 50 percent of weight and resultant revenue because of lorries not being weighed for three to four days.

Now, despite all these (manmade) odds, the small farmer/producer has to repay the loan with interest. And if he[400] cannot, he becomes "untouchable" and gets excluded from the formal system, often never to be re-included again and left to the mercy of "infamous" money lenders. And more often than not, MFIs/banks use the joint liability group mechanism to ensure that the loans taken get paid by guarantors—even when the yield from the sugarcane crop is reduced (due to the unfair actions of other stakeholders) and thereby, income from the crop is insufficient to pay off the loan.

What needs to be noted here is that the interest on the loan starts ticking from when the agreement is signed and/or seeds are supplied to the farmer, whereas the payment is made to the farmer at least three to four months after the crop has been harvested and supplied to the sugar factory. And when you factor the delays in the supply of fertilizer, cutting the crop and/or lifting the cane to the factory, you realize that the sugarcane farmer

---

[400] This is true for all types of small producers, including silk weavers in Kancheepuram or Malda/Murshidabad, different kinds of artisans across India, fishers in the south Indian peninsula and several others.

is a modern day Karna,[401] who is killed many times before the loan (Arjuna) overwhelms him.

In some ways, the above financing arrangement is outrageous, as it penalizes the small producer for mistakes of other parties in the arrangement, which reduces yield and revenue. The fair and obvious thing to do would be to ensure the sharing of risks and costs among the three parties—i.e., the producer, sugar factory and financier. This will enable alignment of incentives and ensure that there is congruence in all actions and inputs.

In fact, Ramaiah's case and that of other similar small farmers/producers has tremendous implications for financial inclusion in this country.

- Financial inclusion is a necessary but not a sufficient condition for better livelihoods. Those who attempt to include the poor and disadvantaged must also pay attention to other factors and risks that can result in the included being ultimately excluded again. This is a significant lesson for those arguing for the financial inclusion of poor-through livelihood financing -as a means rather than an end.

- Finance (livelihood or micro-credit), as it currently exists, is not fair to the client or small producers. Hence, finance must focus on quality servicing and

---

[401] In Mahabharat, a great Indian epic, after Arjuna (of Pandavas) kills Karna (with the Kauravas), he tells Lord Krishna, I am so sorry that I killed my brother. Lord Krishna says that Karna died many times before and what Arjuna did was to merely send a last arrow. Karna was also considered as the epitome of sacrifice and loyalty. The metaphor is used here to show that there are many places where unfair practices do the equivalent to included Indian sugarcane farmers and thereby makes them default on their loans and be ultimately excluded.

attempt to be sensitive to clients" needs and design/deliver products that are fair and useful to them. More improper finance could only be disastrous and this is one of the main reasons why we see a cycle of inclusion and exclusion among low-income clients. In fact, that is why newer programmes are perhaps being initiated time and again, from the days of the erstwhile Integrated Rural Development Programme (IRDP) and the present financial inclusion drive and the National Rural Livelihoods Mission (NRLM).

- Much more than financial inclusion needs to be done to ensure that farmers (and small producers) who put in the effort, make the investment and take the risk, actually get rewards and returns commensurate with their efforts, investment and risk. If this becomes the goal of financial inclusion, then, properly delivered enabling services will automatically become a part of the whole financial inclusion agenda. This indeed has significant implications for the design of the wider financial inclusion programme in terms of what it is doing and what it should be doing. I hope there is honest introspection in this regard, and programmes are tailored accordingly to meet the needs of low-income farmers and producers.

As a beginning, the RBI could take up the cause of low-income sugarcane farmers and producers who perhaps number over 40 million in India. A single client-sensitive financial product would ensure that a large number of low-income people are prevented from being excluded. And the same analysis to ensure fairness to clients can be initiated with a variety of livelihood—related financial products for low-income people. **These, rather than any interest rate subsidy or subvention or loan waiver or any other mechanism, would better serve the cause**

of financial inclusion and inclusive growth. I hope that the RBI focuses on ensuring fairness in financial access which is vital to creating and sustaining inclusive growth in modern day India.

Appendix 9: State-wise Stamp Duty and Registration Fees in India[402]

Table: State-wise Stamp Duty and Registration Fees in India			
States	Criteria	Stamp Duty	Registration Fees
Andhra Pradesh	Sale Deed	4%	0.50%
	Conveyance Deed (gift, mortgage, lease etc.)	5%	0.50%
Maharashtra	Within Municipal Corporation boundary	5%	1%
	Within Municipal Council boundary	4%	1%
	Within Gram Panchayat boundary	3%	1%
Odisha	None	7%	2%
Tamil Nadu	Sale Deed	7%	1%
Karnataka	Conveyance	5%	1%
Goa	None	7%	1%
Gujarat	None	4.90%	1.%
Rajasthan	General	5%	1%
	Male	-	1%
	Female	4%	1%
	Female (SC/ST/BPL)	3%	1%
	Disabled	4%	1%
Punjab	None	6%	1%
Haryana	Sale Deed - Within Municipal boundary	Male – 7% Female – 5%	From Rs 1 – Rs 50,000 It is Rs. 100.
	Sale Deed - Outside Municipal boundary	Male – 5% Female – 3%	From Rs 50,001 – Rs 100,000 it is Rs. 500.
	Conveyance Deed - Within Municipal	7%	From Rs

---

[402] This has been compiled from various websites and state government information sources.

The Cinderella Notes

States	Criteria	Stamp Duty	Registration Fees
	Table: State-wise Stamp Duty and Registration Fees in India		
	boundary		100,001 – Rs 5,00,000 it is Rs. 1,000. From Rs 500,001 – Rs 1,000,000 it is Rs. 5,000. From Rs 1,000,001-Rs 2,000,000 it is Rs. 10,000. From Rs 2,000,001-Rs 2,500,000 it is Rs. 12,500. Above Rs 25 Lakhs it is Rs. 15,000.
	Conveyance Deed - Outside Municipal boundary	5%	
Uttar Pradesh	None	8% additional 2% stamp duty in areas to which U.P. Awas Evam Vikas Parishad Abhiyan is extended (Allahabad, Agra, Kanpur , Lucknow)	2%
Delhi	Sale Deed and Conveyance Deed	Male 6% Female 4%	1%

Table: State-wise Stamp Duty and Registration Fees in India			
States	Criteria	Stamp Duty	Registration Fees
Madhya Pradesh	None	8%	1%
Chhattisgarh	None	7.50%	1%
Jharkhand	Conveyance (Sale Deed)	4%	3%
West Bengal	Within Municipal boundary	6%	1.10%
	Outside Municipal boundary	5%	1.10%
Manipur	None	4%	3%
Sikkim	None	4%	1%

The Cinderella Notes

Appendix 10: Aspects of Copyright

Ramesh S Arunachalam claims copyright only with the original writings, ideas, interpretation, and analysis done by the author, Ramesh S Arunachalam. No copyright is claimed with regard to any material that is quoted. Furthermore, much of the material that is quoted is taken from Statutory Enquiry Commissions. All of these, to the best of my understanding and interpretation of the law, are free of copyright protection. In fact, as per the website of the Office of the Law Revision Counsel United States Code[403] and the website of the United States Copyright office,[404] as per Section, 105,. (Subject matter of copyright: United States Government works), copyright protection (under this title) is not available for any work of the United States Government.

That said, every document that has been quoted has been thoroughly checked for copyright information and none of the documents from which quotes have been taken contain copyright notice either as a symbol © (the letter C in a circle), or the word "Copyright," or the abbreviation "Copr." There is no name of the owner, no abbreviation by which the name can be recognized, no generally known alternative designation of the owner, nor any indication of an owner of any copyright in these government works. Therefore, in the absence of the copyright notice and copyright owner information and as per Sections 105 and 403 of the Copyright Laws of the

---

[403]Office of the Law Revision Counsel United States Code, 17 USC: Subject Matter of Copyright: United States Government works, http://uscode.house.gov/view.xhtml?req=%28title:17%20section:10 5%20edition:prelim%29

[404] Copyright Law of the United States of America and Related Laws Contained in Title 17 of the *United States Code*, Section 105, Subject Matter of Copyright: United States Government works, http://www.copyright.gov/title17/92chap1.html#105

United States, it can only be inferred that these government reports, orders, releases etc. (representing work of the United States federal government), are not protected by copyright.

Likewise, the concerned websites have either stated that "information on State Department websites is in the public domain and may be copied and distributed without permission,"[405] or they have stated that "all of the content of the website constitutes a work of the United States federal government under sections 105[406] and 403[407] of title 17 of the U.S. Code,"[408] which again frees the information from copyright protection.

[405] U.S. Department of State, Copyright Information, http://www.state.gov/misc/87529.htm#copyright
[406] Subject Matter of Copyright: United States Government works, U.S Code 105.
[407] Copyright Law of the United States of America and Related Laws Contained in Title 17 of the *United States Code,* Section 403, Notice of copyright: Publications incorporating United States Government works, http://www.copyright.gov/title17/92chap4.html
[408] The Select Committee on Benghazi, Copyright, https://benghazi.house.gov/copyright.

About the Author

Ramesh S Arunachalam wears many hats. He is an Industrial Engineer from the National Institute of Technology (NIT), Trichy, India and an MBA (with Dual Concentration, Strategy and Marketing) from the Carlson School of Management, University of Minnesota, Minneapolis, USA. In the last 30 years, he has been a columnist with the Hindu Business Line (1995-97) and Moneylife (2011-2013), a development practitioner and strategic advisor. He has worked in a wide range of areas including financial sector regulation and supervision, financial inclusion, microfinance, livelihoods and MSMEs, Gender and microfinance, ERP systems for microfinance and infrastructure finance, urban development, infrastructure financing, GIS for urban planning and e Governance.

During the last 30 years, Ramesh has completed over 260 professional assignments. He has worked in 570 districts of India and has also travelled and worked extensively in over 25 countries in North America, Asia, Africa, Europe and the Caribbean across diverse projects (in senior positions). He is passionate about his work and brings strong inter-disciplinary insight to his assignments. His clients include governments (Governments of India, St Lucia, Singapore, Malawi, Uganda, Philippines, Afghanistan etc, several State Governments in India and many GoI Institutions like NCRPB, SIDBI, NABARD etc), bi-lateral agencies (DFID, USAID, DANIDA, NORAD, SIDA etc), multi-lateral agencies (UNDP, World Bank, ADB, IFAD, The Commonwealth Secretariat etc), regulators, commercial banks, investment banks, microfinance institutions, private sector firms and several other stakeholders globally. He has authored numerous reports/studies/papers as part of his assignments, several of which have been published internationally and received global recognition. His blog on microfinance has been well received and he has also penned two books in microfinance and financial inclusion—**The Journey of Indian Microfinance: Lessons for the Future** and **An Idea Which Went Wrong: Commercial Microfinance in India**—both of which have received critical acclaim. His first novel is an entertaining crime thriller—**Where Angels Prey**—released in April 2015 through AuthorsUpFront, which again was well received. His non-fiction writing continued in 2016 with critically acclaimed popular books—**"Madam President: History in the Making?"** and **"Dirty Money: The U.S. Presidential Elections 2016"** (see www.amazon.com)

Title – **Where Angels Prey**
Author – Ramesh S Arunachalam
Size – 5.5 inches × 8.5 inches
No of Pages – 204
Binding – Paperback
ISBN – 978-9384439378

While the rest of the world reels under a severe financial crisis, India's microfinance sector enjoys an unprecedented boom. Why on earth are people investing such huge amounts of money in an obscure industry, especially at the time of global recession? And why is Wall Street suddenly so interested in India's poor?

That is exactly what Robert Bradlee, senior correspondent with *The New York Post*, sets off to investigate, along with his journalist friend, Chandresh. Little does he know that his search for a scoop would lead him through a complex multi-pronged web of deceit, fraud, manipulation and financial crime, remote controlled from distant lands by an entire chain of financial sector stakeholders.

Gripping, racy and meticulously researched, this financial thriller weaves in and out of the affluent world of high-powered boardrooms and the gruelling poverty of the remotest villages of India, to reveal the devastating truths that often lurk behind "good intentions".